English Men of Letters

EDITED BY JOHN MORLEY

GEORGE ELIOT

AMS PRESS

NEW YORK

GEORGE ELIOT

BY

LESLIE STEPHEN

New York

THE MACMILLAN COMPANY

LONDON: MACMILLAN & CO., Ltd.

1902

Library of Congress Cataloging in Publication Data

Stephen, Sir Leslie, 1832–1904.
   George Eliot.

   Original ed. issued in series: English men of
letters.
   1. Eliot, George, pseud, i.e. Marian Evans,
afterwards Cross, 1819–1880.
PR4681.S7   1973   823'.8   71–148308
ISBN 0–404–08913–5

Reprinted from the edition of 1902, New York
First AMS edition published in 1973
Manufactured in the United States of America

AMS PRESS INC.
NEW YORK, N. Y.   10003

CONTENTS

CHAPTER VIII

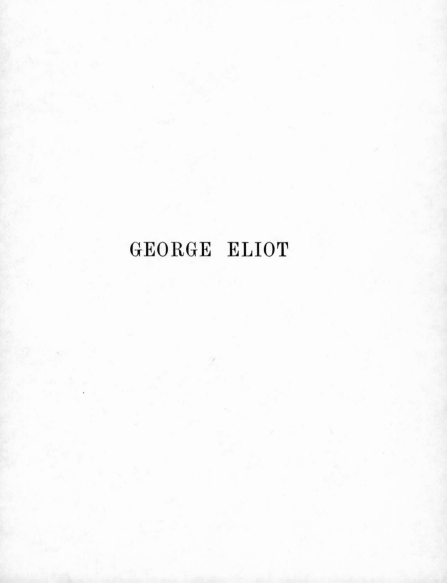

GEORGE ELIOT

GEORGE ELIOT

CHAPTER I

EARLY LIFE

MARY ANN EVANS, as her father recorded in his diary, was born at Arbury Farm, at five o'clock in the morning of 22nd November 1819.[1] Her father, Robert Evans, was son of George Evans, a builder and carpenter in Derbyshire. The family had migrated thither from Northop in Flintshire. Robert Evans was brought up to his father's business, and improved his position by remarkable qualities. He possessed great vigour both of mind and body, and was one of the men to whom love of good work is a religion. Once, when two labourers were waiting for a third to enable them to carry a heavy ladder, he took the whole weight upon his own shoulders, and astonished them by carrying it to its destination without help. He had also the keen eye of a skilful workman, and was especially famous for a power of calculating with singular accuracy the quantity of timber in a standing tree. He acquired the highest character for integrity and thorough devotion to his employers' interests. His extensive knowledge in very varied practical

[1] She called herself Marian.

B   1

departments, as his daughter says, "made his services valued through several counties. He had large knowledge of mines, of plantations, of various branches of valuation and measurement — of all that is essential to the management of large estates." He was regarded as a unique land-agent, and was able by giving his own services to save the special fees usually paid by landowners for expert opinions. His education had been imperfect, and this led to some self-distrust and "submissiveness in his domestic relations." The last peculiarity is reflected in the character of Mr. Garth in *Middlemarch;* and Mr. Garth and Adam Bede are obviously in some degree representative of the same type — one, it is to be feared, which has not become commoner since his time. About 1799 Robert Evans was agent to Mr. Francis Newdigate of Kirk Hallam in Derbyshire, under whom he also held a farm. In 1806, upon the death of Sir Roger Newdigate, Francis Newdigate inherited a life interest in the Arbury estate in Warwickshire, and Evans accompanied him thither in his old capacity. Colonel Newdigate, son of Francis, was much impressed by the merits of his father's agent, and through the colonel's influence Evans became agent to various other great landowners in the district. As became his position, Robert Evans was a sturdy Tory. He shared the patriotic sentiment of the days of Nelson and Wellington, and held that a revolutionary fanatic was a mixture of fool and scoundrel. "I was accustomed," says his daughter, "to hear him utter the word 'Government' in a tone that charged it with awe and made it part of my effective religion in contrast with the word 'rebel,' which seemed to carry the stamp of evil in its syllables, and, lit by the fact that Satan was the first rebel, made an argument dispensing with more detailed inquiry." "Government," for practical purposes, meant the great landowners, who had good reasons for returning his respect. One of them requires a moment's notice.

Sir Roger Newdigate,[1] the previous owner of Arbury, was a typical specimen of the more cultivated country gentleman of his day. In early life he had made the "grand tour," and had brought back ancient marbles and architectural drawings. He afterwards accepted the active duties of his position. He represented the University of Oxford for thirty years (1750–1780) as a high Tory. He was an owner of collieries and a promoter of canals. He built a school and a poorhouse for the parish in which Arbury Park is situated — Chilvers-Coton, near Nuneaton. He rebuilt Arbury House, which stood on the site of an ancient priory, in the "Gothic style" and adorned it with works of art and family portraits by Romney and Reynolds. His name at least is familiar to all Oxford men by the prize poem which he founded just before his death. The conditions prescribed by him for the competition show as much sense as can be expected from the founder of a prize poem. There were to be no compliments to himself, and the length of the poems was to be limited to fifty lines. Horace and King David, as he remarked, had succeeded in confining their noblest compositions within that length, and the quality of the future prize poems would probably not be such as to make us desire more of them than of

[1] See *The Cheverels of Cheverel Manor*, by Lady Newdigate-Newdegate, 1898.

the psalms or odes. Sir Roger died thirteeen years before the birth of Evans's daughter; but certain family stories in which he was concerned were handed down to her, and, as we shall see, suggested one of her most finished pieces of work. Robert Evans's first wife, Harriet Poynton, had been for " many years," as her epitaph says, " the friend and servant of the family of Arbury." She had married Evans in 1801, and died in 1809, leaving two children. In 1813 Evans married a woman of rather superior position, Christiana Pearson, by whom he had three children — Christiana, Isaac, and Mary Ann — Christiana being about five, and Isaac about three years older than the youngest child. In March 1820, when Mary Ann was four months old, the Evanses moved to Griff, "a charming red brick, ivy-covered house on the Arbury estate." It was to be the child's home for the first twenty-one years of her life.

The impressions made upon the girl during these years are sufficiently manifest in the first series of her novels. Were it necessary to describe the general characteristics of English country life, they would enable the " graphic " historian to give life and colour to the skeleton made from statistical and legal information. The *Scenes of Clerical Life, Adam Bede, Silas Marner,* and *The Mill on the Floss,* probably give the most vivid picture now extant of the manners and customs of the contemporary dwellers in the midland counties of England. There is a temptation to press the likeness further. It is a favourite amusement of readers to identify characters in novels with historical individuals. They sometimes seem to think that the question whether (for example) Caleb Garth

" was " Robert Evans can be answered by a simple
Yes or No, like the question whether Junius was
Philip Francis. In reality, of course, it is generally
impossible to say precisely how far the portrait may
have been studied from a single model, or modified
intentionally, or by blending with more or less conscious reminiscences of other originals. George Eliot
(as it will be convenient to call her hereafter from
her name in letters), like all good novelists, generally
avoided direct delineation of individuals; while, on
the other hand, it is probable enough that she was
sometimes following the facts more closely than she
was herself aware. It is enough to say here that her
mother had a " considerable dash of the Mrs. Poyser
vein in her " ; that her mother's family more or less
stood for the Dodsons in the *Mill on the Floss;* that
her relations to her brother resembled those of Maggie
to Tom Tulliver in the same novel; and that when
describing Celia and Dorothea Brooke in *Middlemarch*
she was more or less recalling her relations to her
elder sister Christiana. There is one person, however,
whom a novelist can hardly help revealing directly or
indirectly; and in the case of George Eliot the revelation is unequivocal. There is no doubt, as we shall
see, that the *Mill on the Floss* is substantially autobiographical, not, of course, a statement of facts, but
as a vivid embodiment of the early impressions and
the first stages of spiritual development. The scanty
framework of fact may be partly filled up from this
source.

It is proper, however, at the present day to begin
from the physical " environment " of the organism
whose history we are to study. The Warwickshire

landscape is not precisely stimulating: and if the county can boast of the greatest name in English literature, it must be remembered that Shakespeare had the good fortune to migrate to the centre of intellectual activity at an early period. Though the central watershed of England passes through the country, it has no mountain ridges, and the streams crawl off through modest undulations to more picturesque districts. In her twenty-first year George Eliot speaks of a little excursion in which she has (for the first time apparently) "gazed on some — albeit the smallest — of the 'everlasting hills,'" and has admired "those noblest children of the earth — fine healthy trees." She has seen, too, a fine parish church and Lichfield Cathedral. Through her childhood she had to put up with canals instead of rivers; and saw no wilder open spaces than the decorous lawns of Arbury Park. Far away in the north, the Brontë children — of whom Charlotte, the eldest, was her senior by three years—were spending their strange childhood in Haworth, learning to worship Nature on the Yorkshire moors, and to idealise the sturdy, crabbed, North-countrymen into Rochesters and Heathcliffs. We may speculate if we please upon the effects which might have followed if the habitats of the two families could have been exchanged. If we may trust their portrayers, the fat midland pastures were hardly more different from the Yorkshire moors than the stolid farmers of Warwickshire from the rough population of the West Riding.

"Our midland plains," said George Eliot, "have never lost their familiar expression and conservative spirit for me; yet at every other mile, since I first

looked on them, some sign of world-wide change, some
new direction of human labour, has wrought itself
into what one may call the speech of the landscape."
The scenery, a monotonous succession of little ups
and downs, is of the kind which owes its interest
to its subordination to human society. In George
Eliot's writings, there are proofs enough of sensibility
to natural beauty, but the scenery is a background to
the actors ; and there is no indication of such a passion
for her native district as Scott felt for his " honest grey
hills." The "midland plains " were " conservative,"
because they spoke of ancient order and peace; and
the opening pages of *Felix Holt* describe the scenery and
explain its significance. The traveller of those days,
seated by the side of one of Mr. Weller's colleagues,
whirling at the amazing speed of ten miles an hour
across the plain whence the waters flow to the Avon
and the Trent, had yet time to read many indications
of English life in the characteristic landscape. He
saw broad meadows with their long lines of willows
marking the water-courses ; and cornfields divided by
the straggling hedgerows, economically wasteful but
beautiful with their bushes of hawthorn and dog-roses.
He came upon remote hamlets, abodes of dirt and
ignorance, each knowing of the world which lay beyond
its "own patch of earth and sky " only by intercourse
with " big, bold, gin-breathing tramps." But at times
also he passed through " trim cheerful villages," where
the cottage gardens bloomed with wall-flowers and
geraniums, and the blacksmith and the wheelwright
were plying their cheerful trades. Solid farmers were
jogging past from their comfortable homesteads, where
quaint yew-tree arbours were backed by the great

cornstacks. At intervals appeared the squires' state-
lier mansions, embowered in the patrician trees of his
park, and hard by the grey old churches with sleep-
compelling pews were the parsonages where the
squire's younger son was quartered, not yet prescient
of the "movement," and free at least from "too
much zeal." In such districts the eighteenth century
calm lingered pleasantly, and the ideal types represented by Sir Roger de Coverley and the Vicar of
Wakefield, or by Squire Western and Trulliber, might
still be recognised. A Sir Roger Newdigate had acquired a taste, and here and there clerical calm was
being ruffled by Evangelical or Methodist agitation.
But the district was one of "protuberant optimists, sure
that Old England was the best of all possible countries,
and that if there were any facts which had not fallen
under their own observation they were facts not worth
observing." The traveller, it is true, might soon come
upon a very different scene. The coach would emerge
from the deep-rutted lanes into a village "dingy with
coal-dust, noisy with the shaking of looms," or "would
rattle over the pavement of a manufacturing town,
the scene of riots and trade-union meetings." The
land around him was blackened with coal-pits, and
the population was by no means convinced that all
change must be for the worse ; and yet these busy
scenes seemed "to make but crowded nests in the
midst of the large-spaced, slow-moving life of home-
stead and far-away cottages and oak-sheltered parks."
In the quiet agricultural region, squire and parson,
and the whole social machinery of which they represented the mainspring, could still be accepted as part
of the unalterable system of things. The villager

was too ignorant even to conceive the possibility of change; and if the farmer grumbled over the ruinous results of peace, he retained his traditional reverence for the old families, and looked with horror upon proposals for the intrusion of railways or manufacturing demands for free trade. If the upper social stratum was aware that in the great towns there were Radicals demanding the abolition of the House of Lords and the confiscation of Church property, it inferred that the demon of revolution had not been completely exorcised, but could still hope that, with the help of the great Duke, the evil spirit might be confined to his proper region, and the British Constitution be upheld as the pride and envy of the world.

In due time George Eliot was to portray various phases of the society around her, including the Radical as well as the fine old Tory. In her childhood, of course, she took the colouring of her surroundings. To the infant the arrangements of its nursery are as unalterable as the laws of the solar system and the existence of any other order inconceivable. Her world was the fireside of Griff; and if she had glimpses of the outside, the views of Mr. Robert Evans represented ultimate truth, or were taken as indisputable assertions of matter of fact. He was fond of his little girl, and took her for occasional outings in his gig, or on expeditions to neighbouring country towns. The family circle was small. Soon after her birth, her mother's health became weak; the elder girl, Christiana, was sent to school; and Mary Ann with her brother spent part of every day at a dame-school close to their own gates. She did not show any remarkable precocity, though she was both a thoughtful and a very affec-

tionate and sensitive child. Her brother became
naturally the first object of her devotion, and devotion
to some one was throughout her life a marked need of
her nature. While still under five years old, she went
through the experiences more or less idealised in the
Mill on the Floss, and more historically commemorated
in the series of sonnets called *Brother and Sister*. She
tells in the poems how she rambled with him through
the meadows; across the rivulet hidden by tangled
forget-me-nots; through the rookery and by the
"brown canal," where the barges seemed to bring
intimations of an unknown world beyond. In the
copse, there were traces of the "mystic gypsies,"
where Mr. Petulengro perhaps had encamped, though
when she actually met him — if the narrative in the
Mill on the Floss be authentic history — he was a less
romantic being than we should judge from his behaviour in *Lavengro*. Then, too, she had the wonderful
adventure of catching a perch by mistake, which suggests the inevitable moral, namely, that "luck was
with glory wed." The early hero-worship of the little
girl running like a puppy after the slightly bigger
brother is simply and touchingly described. "School
parted us," she says; and she never found that childish world again.

> ' But were another childish world my share,
> I would be born a little sister there.'

Her brother was sent to school when she was five
years old; and as her mother was still in bad health,
she was sent to join her sister at a school kept by a
Miss Lathom at Attleboro, a village only a mile or two
distant from Griff. She continued there for three or
four years, spending her Sundays at home. Her chief

memory of this part of her life was the difficulty of
getting a seat near the fireplace in cold weather. Her
health was low, it seems, and she suffered from the
nightly terrors which haunt delicate children, and which
she has ascribed to Gwendolen Harleth. "All her
soul," she said, "became a quivering fear." The other
pupils, however, made a pet of their small companion,
and she was not unhappy. She began to read such
books as then came in the way of children. In one of
them, called *The Linnet's Life*, she afterwards wrote a
few words, stating that it was the first present from
her father which she could remember, and recording
her early delight in its pages. She remembered, too,
her absorption in *Æsop's Fables*, and laughed heartily
over the pleasure she had taken in the humour of
"Mercury and the Statue Seller." A stray volume of
Joe Miller supplied her with anecdotes wherewith to
astonish her family. In those days children were less
distracted by miscellaneous scraps of print, and could
pore over the same thumbed and dogs-eared favourites.
In her eighth or ninth year she was sent to a larger
school, kept by a Miss Wallington at Nuneaton. Here
there were some thirty boarders, and she became especially intimate with Miss Lewis, the principal governess.
Her passion for reading developed rapidly. A stray
Waverley came in her way; and when that was returned
to its owner before she had finished it, she began
writing out the story for herself, till her elders got it
back for her. She was fascinated by an extract from
Lamb's *Captain Jackson* even in an almanac; and among
her favourite books were Defoe's *History of the Devil*,
Pilgrim's Progress, and *Rasselas*. By this time it was
beginning to be understood that there was something

remarkable about the child. She excited the admiration of the home circle by acting charades with her brother during the holidays; and if not a decided "prodigy," was clearly capable of absorbing such intellectual influences as could be found in Warwickshire. In her thirteenth year she was transferred to a school at Coventry. It was kept by two ladies named Franklin, daughters of a Baptist minister, who had for many years preached in a chapel at Coventry. He lived in a house "almost exactly resembling that of Rufus Lyon in *Felix Holt*." Lyon's character and some of his little personal peculiarities were also suggested by this original. George Eliot was always grateful to the daughters for the excellence of their teaching. She was at once recognised as the most promising of their pupils. Her themes were kept for the private edification of her teachers, instead of being read in the class like those of her comrades. She had good masters in French and German and music. She was sometimes called upon to display her musical skill before visitors, as the best performer in the school; and obeyed with ready good humour, though suffering agonies of shyness. The love of music generally shows itself at an early age, but she had apparently some difficulty in yielding to the passion. Three years after leaving school, she attended an oratorio at Coventry, and says in a letter that she thinks it will be her last. She declares that she has "no soul for music," and is a "tasteless person." She therefore is not qualified to discuss the question of the "propriety or lawfulness of such exhibitions of talent." For herself, she would not regret if music were strictly confined to purposes of worship; and cannot think that "a pleasure that wishes the devotion of all the time and powers of an immortal being to the acquirement of an expertness in so useless . . . an accomplishment can be quite pure and elevating in its tendency." The religious theory is, as we shall see, characteristic; but it is singular that a woman who was to find one of her greatest delights in music, and who was already skilled in the art, should think herself devoid of the capacity. Two years later, indeed, she was moved to "hysterical sobbing" by another oratorio. She was always diffident and easily discouraged; and these reflections may mean merely an attack of low spirits. Perhaps the want of "soul" meant only the absence of a specific aptitude for the musician's calling; or, possibly, the singing at Coventry was out of tune.[1]

George Eliot left school finally at the end of 1835. Her mother was failing in health, and died in the summer of 1836, after a long illness, during which she was nursed by her daughters. In the following spring the elder daughter, Christiana, married Mr. Edward Clarke, a surgeon in Warwickshire, and Mary Ann undertook the charge of her father's household at Griff. She set her mind to the work, and became, it is said, an "exemplary housewife." She also exerted herself in promoting various charitable works, and continued to study Italian, German, and music. Her brother was now beginning to take a share in their father's busi-

[1] Mr. W. A. White of New York has kindly shown me a letter to another friend in which George Eliot speaks of the same oratorio. It might be urged, she admits, that such exhibitions show "the beautiful powers of the human voice when carried to the highest point of improveability." But such reasoning would compel us to admit "opera-dancing, horse-racing, and even intemperance."

ness ; and found his chief relaxation from hard work in hunting — an amusement which was not in his sister's line. He had also become a High Churchman, whereas she was strongly Evangelical. Although, therefore, the family was bound by ties of warm affection, she found little sympathy in her favourite occupations. She lived in intellectual solitude, conscious of abilities for which she could find no definite outlet, and with no one in her immediate circle capable of guiding or even appreciating her pursuits. When long afterwards an autobiography was suggested to her, she replied : " The only thing I should much care to dwell on [in regard to this period] would be the absolute despair I suffered from of ever being able to do anything. No one could ever have felt greater despair, and a knowledge of this might be a help to some other struggler." On the other hand, she added with a smile, " it might only lead to an increase of bad writing."

The account of George Eliot's school days may perhaps suggest that the state of female education in Warwickshire was not altogether so bad as energetic modern reformers are apt to assume. There is, it is true, something of a quaint old-fashioned colouring about the system. Her comrades at Miss Franklin's thought that she was competent "to get up something in the way of a clothing club "; and beyond that limited prospect, they may possibly have dared to hope that she might develop into a Mrs. Chapone or Miss Carter — capable of writing letters "upon the improvement of the human mind," or possibly, in time, of translating Epictetus. She was not, indeed, competent to take a first-class in a University examination, or to enter any career for which such honours qualified the

nobler sex; and yet, if we really believed what we are
so often told, that the test of a good education is not
the stock of knowledge acquired, but the stimulus
given to mental activity, the schooling seems to have
been successful enough. Her intellectual curiosity
was roused, though not yet fixed upon any definite
object. From the correspondence which she kept up
with her early governess, Miss Lewis, it seems that
she read a great deal of miscellaneous literature during
sixteen years at Griff. My mind, she says in 1839,
presents "an assemblage of disjointed specimens of
history, ancient and modern; scraps of poetry picked
up from Shakespeare, Cowper, Wordsworth, and
Milton; newspaper topics; morsels of Addison and
Bacon, Latin verbs, geometry, entomology, and chem-
istry; Reviews and metaphysics — all arrested and
petrified and smothered by the fast-thickening every-
day accession of actual events, relative anxieties, and
household cares and vexations. How deplorably and
unaccountably evanescent are our frames of mind, as
various as forms and hues of the summer clouds!"
For a girl of nineteen, both the style and the variety
of intellectual interests indicated are remarkable. A
genius, it may be suggested, can thrive anywhere;
and so long as it is not absolutely fettered, can derive
nourishment from any set of materials that may come
in its way. There is, however, a special characteristic
of George Eliot which already appears. A strong
imaginative impulse is generally developed early; it
is an overmastering faculty which forces its possessor
into activity often before knowledge or serious thought
has accumulated; draws romances, epic poems, and
dramas from children in their teens; and suggests

that not only the material surroundings, but even the storage of intellectual accomplishments is but an accidental stimulus to the innate creative power. Charlotte and Emily Brontë, for example, informed the world around them with so much passion and imagination, that we fancy that any other circumstances would have served for an incentive to powers only waiting to be set at liberty. George Eliot, diffident in character, and reflective as much as imaginative in intellect, developed slowly, and was for many years ignorant of her own truest powers. She had a full share of the feminine docility, which is so charming to teachers — especially of the other sex. Women really enjoy lectures, strange as the taste appears to the male at all ages. Even a clever boy generally regards his schoolmaster as a natural enemy, and begins as a rebel. The girl takes the master at his own valuation, or something more, and has an innocent belief that lessons give really desirable information. George Eliot was clearly of this way of thinking; and though she must have been aware of possessing unusual ability, she was anxious to bow submissively to the best instructors. At Griff or in her circle at Coventry no very brilliant intellectual light was shining, nor did even a very clear understanding prevail as to the real lights of contemporary thought. People had not taken to reading the last German authorities; and had vague enough impressions as to the course of European speculation. Miss Lewis and the Miss Franklins were ardent Evangelicals; and the Evangelical school of the day, though not given to philosophy, representing at least the most socially active party in the Church, was so far attractive to her

intellectually. It meant at any rate a protest against
stagnation. Then, moreover, through life she had
very deep religious sentiments, and for the present
associated them with the Evangelical dogma. She
was greatly impressed by the wife of her father's
younger brother, Mrs. Samuel Evans, a Methodist
preacher, of whom I shall presently have to speak
again. " I shall not only suffer, but be delighted to
receive the word of exhortation," she writes to her
aunt in 1839, " and I beg you not to withhold it."
The most curious of her letters in these years is one
to Miss Lewis, discussing with a quaint gravity the
ethics of reading fiction. She is good enough to admit
that certain standard works must be read — Scott, for
example, and Don Quixote — otherwise one would
not understand common allusions. Shakespeare, too,
is inevitable, though one must be as nice as the bee
" to suck nothing but honey from his pages." A
teacher, too, may consider it desirable to read fiction
by way of tasting for her pupils. But it is dangerous
to make trial on oneself of a cup because it is suspected
of being poisonous. She herself has suffered from the
poison. Her early reading of novels, lent by kind
friends, led her to castle-building, which she apparently thinks a pernicious habit. No one, of course,
" ever dreamed of recommending " novels to children ;
but men and women are but children of a larger
growth. They cannot be sure at any age of resisting
the evil influences. Nothing can be learned from
novels which cannot be better learned from history ;
and when she is driven to tears by the impossibility
of learning more than a fraction of realities, can
she " have any time to spend on things that never

c

existed " ?   It is plain that in those days æsthetic
prophets had not begun to expound the true relations
of art and morality ; and many young ladies of nineteen at the present day would consider themselves
competent to open the eyes of this didactic young
person.   Her views changed in good time ; but the
moral earnestness which prompted these rather crude
remarks was a permanent characteristic.   Meanwhile,
if her scruples hindered her from acquiring a wide
knowledge upon the novels of the day, she was
spending her time to better purpose in the miscellaneous reading already noticed.   Wordsworth, it may
be observed, was an early favourite to whom she
remained faithful through life, and appealed to her
as, shortly before, he had appealed, though still more
strongly, to J. S. Mill.   She was much impressed, too,
by Young's *Night Thoughts*, an edifying work which
in later years she criticised with the severity of a
revolted disciple.   Her studies naturally took a theological direction.   She begins with Hannah More and
Wilberforce, and is presently interested by the controversies aroused by the Oxford movement.   She cannot make up her mind as to the solution.   She reads
an essay on " Schism " by Professor Hoppus of the
London University, and the Evangelical Milner's *Church
History*.   She compares their views with those of *The
Portrait of an English Churchman*, by W. Gresley, an
early champion of " Tractarianism," and finds that the
Tracts themselves show a " confused appreciation of
the great doctrine of justification."   They approach
too nearly to the Church marked by the " prophetical
epithets " of " the scarlet beast " and the " Mystery of
Iniquity."   The authors, it is true, are zealous, learned,

and devoted, but "Satan is too crafty to commit his
cause into the hands of those who have nothing to
recommend them to approbation." She is pleased,
however, by the *Lyra Apostolica* and the "sweet
poetry" of the *Christian Year*. She is presently much
impressed by the work upon *Ancient Christianity and
the Oxford Tracts*, by Isaac Taylor, "one of the most
eloquent, acute, and pious of writers." She has
"gulped it in a most reptile-like fashion," but must
"*chew* it thoroughly to facilitate its assimilation
with her mental frame." She is attracted, too, by
the "stirring eloquence" of *The Great Teacher*, written
by John Harris, a popular writer of the time, with
liberal tendencies, who was afterwards principal of
an Independent College. These studies, it must be
remembered, represent her state of mind before the
completion of her twenty-first year. She was soon
to come under new influences. Meanwhile she was
already ambitious enough to propose to make a
practical application of her reading, and planned a
"chart" of ecclesiastical history, with columns showing the dates of the principal personages, events,
schisms, and so forth, with perhaps one for the
fulfilment of the prophecies. Happily a chart was
published by some one else which extinguished hers,
and she turned to other studies. A different result of
her meditations was a poem, which, though not her first
attempt at poetry, was the first published. It is a farewell to the world, of which this is a specimen : —

> " Books that have been to me as chests of gold,
>   Which, miserlike, I secretly have told,
>   And for them love, health, friendship, peace have sold,
>   Farewell !

Blest Volume ! whose clear truth-writ page once known
Fades not before heaven's sunshine and hell's moan,
To thee I say not, of earth's gifts alone,

Farewell !

Then shall my new-born senses find new joy,
New sounds, new sights, my ears and eyes employ,
Nor fear that word that here brings sad alloy,

Farewell ! "

The editor of the *Christian Observer*, in which the
lines appeared (January 1840), adds a note to the
effect that in heaven we shall be able to do without
the Bible. The verses, however, if suspected of this
trifling heresy, show religious feeling much more
distinctly than poetical power, in which they resemble
most sacred poetry.

CHAPTER II

When George Eliot was just twenty-one a change took place in her life which was to produce most important results. Her brother had married, and it was arranged that he should take over his father's business at Griff. Mr. Robert Evans, now sixty-six, with his daughter migrated to Coventry. They took a semi-detached house in the Foleshill Road, with a "good bit of garden round it," and commanding a wide reach of country, though the view was disfigured by mills and chimneys in the foreground. The secluded agricultural district was exchanged for an energetic manufacturing town, and George Eliot was gaining a new set of experiences, to be turned to account in good time. Hitherto her life had been one of intellectual isolation, though she had been encouraged by the sympathy of Miss Lewis. She had aspirations as well as reflections, and complains to her Methodist aunt that her "besetting sin was ambition — a desire insatiable for the esteem of my fellow-creatures. This seems the centre whence all my actions proceed." But the powers of which she was conscious were choked in the confined atmosphere where men, as Johnson's friend complained, talked of "runts," that is (according to Boswell) young cows. Dr. Johnson, replied an

21

admirer, would learn to talk of runts. George Eliot
certainly listened to the talk, and then or in memory
could perceive its humorous aspect; but talk confined to
runts becomes tiresome in the long run; and when her
loftiest hope was to compile a historical chart, she must
have felt a painful need for some better end for her
energies. Some one who would share her interests and
direct her aspirations was obviously desirable if she was
to escape from the diffident "despair" into which she
was tempted to sink. Coventry could hardly be described, I imagine, as a Warwickshire Athens, or even
Edinburgh; but at Coventry, as it happened, there were
some people of much wider outlook than could have been
expected. Charles Bray (1811–1884) was a ribbon manu-
facturer and a man of energy and philanthropic aims.
He was a disciple of George Combe the phrenologist,
whose *Constitution of Man* had a great influence at this
time, though not much recognised by the authoritative
expounders of philosophy. Bray himself in 1841 published *The Philosophy of Necessity,* intended to apply
Combe's scientific principles to the regeneration of
society. Like George and Andrew Combe, he sympathised with Robert Owen the Socialist, and took a
special interest in the attempt to found a community
at Queenwood. Upon its failure he took a part in
less ambitious schemes for the improvement of the
working classes. In 1836 Bray married Caroline,
sister of Charles and Sara Hennell. The Hennells had
been brought up as Unitarians; and after his sister's
marriage to Bray, a thoroughgoing sceptic, Charles
Hennell undertook to examine the evidences of Christianity with a view to meeting his brother-in-law's
objections. The result of the examination was that he

became a sceptic himself, and in 1838 published an *Enquiry concerning the Origin of Christianity* in defence of his conclusions. The book is intended to show that Christianity is explicable by purely natural causes. A criticism of the New Testament narrative leads to the conclusion that Jesus was a man of high moral genius, who belonged originally to the sect of the Essenes, and developed their teaching under the influence of the time. Strauss, whose *Life of Christ* had appeared in 1835, procured a translation of Hennell's book into German; and in a preface says that Hennell, although ignorant of recent German criticism, was " on the very track " which the Germans had entered. He had, too, the practical insight of an English man of business, and solved " at one spring " problems over which the German " flutters with many learned formulæ." Hennell treated the subject in the " earnest and dignified tone of the truthseeker " ; and, unlike rancorous assailants of Christianity, derived religion, not from priestcraft, but from the essential needs of human nature. George Eliot's admiration for the book is shown by an analysis [1] which she wrote on the occasion of its republication in 1852. She bought a copy soon after going to Coventry, and had read it before she met the Brays. Kingsley mentions it as one of the books which Alton Locke studied as a representative of the "intelligent artisans of the period." Hennell's sister Sara was interested in the same questions, and expounded her doctrines at length in *Present Religion as a Faith owning Fellowship with Thought.* It appeared in three volumes in 1865, 1873, and 1887, and is one of the many attempts to present

[1] Given in *Life*, i. 76–83.

a philosophical theism in consistence with scientific
thought by the help of a doctrine of evolution. I am
not qualified to speak of its philosophical merits on
the strength of a very superficial inspection, but it is
plain that Miss Hennell had read and reflected sufficiently to be accepted by George Eliot as a valuable
ally in the sphere of philosophical speculation. Her
decided theism led her to criticise Comte with a
hostility which separated her opinions from those of
her friend. They continued, however, to correspond
with mutual respect and affection.

The Evanses' house in Coventry was next door to
that occupied by Mrs. Pears, a sister of Mr. Bray.
An acquaintance with her neighbour Mrs. Pears soon
ripened into friendship, and led in November 1841 to
an introduction to the Brays. A very warm friendship
sprang up. Cara and Sara (Mrs. Bray and Miss
Hennell) became as sisters to George Eliot, and Mr.
Bray her most intimate male friend. The alliance
lasted through life, and produced an important correspondence. The effect upon George Eliot's mental
development was immediate and remarkable. The
little circle at Coventry introduced her to a new
world of thought. It became clear that there were
regions of speculation into which her respected governess Miss Lewis and her beloved aunt Mrs. Samuel
Evans had never entered. A letter to Miss Lewis of
13th November 1841 indicates the change which had
come over her, and apparently refers to a recent study
of Bray's *Enquiry*. "My whole soul," she says, "has
been engrossed in the most interesting of all inquiries
for the last few days, and to what result my thoughts
will lead I know not — possibly to one that will startle

you; but my only desire is to know the truth, my
only fear to cling to error." She hopes that their
"love will not discompose under the influence of
separation." "What a pity," she says to the same
correspondent a few days later, "that while mathematics are indubitable, immutable, and no one doubts
the properties of a triangle or a circle, doctrines infi-
nitely important to man are buried in a charnel heap
of bones, over which nothing is heard but the barks
and growls of contention." The change of belief thus
indicated appears to have been rapid, though there
are indications of previous doubts as to her childish
creed. By January 1842 it had led to a refusal to go
to church, and a consequent family difficulty. It is
not surprising that George Eliot should have followed
a path which was being taken by many contemporaries;
but something must be said of her special position,
which was in many ways characteristic. The chief
light upon her conversion—if I may use the phrase—
comes from another source. George Eliot had been
introduced to a family named Sibree by her old school-
mistress, Miss Franklin, and came to entertain a high
regard for several of its members. The Sibrees were
of the Evangelical persuasion. A son, Mr. John Sibree,
went to a German university in 1842, and afterwards
translated Hegel's *Philosophy of History*, a fact apparently implying that the Brays were not the only inhabitants of Coventry with some taste for philosophical
speculation. George Eliot took a fancy to a daughter,
Miss Mary Sibree, then a young girl, gave her German
lessons, and "talked freely on all subjects," without
attempting "directly to unsettle her Evangelical beliefs." Miss Sibree (afterwards Mrs. John Cash) pre-

served some interesting records of the intercourse,
which show that the change of opinions, if rapid, was
not unprepared. Till she left Griff, George Eliot had
still used the religious language of her own circle.
But the studies which have already been mentioned
had raised doubts. Isaac Taylor's book, which she proposed to "assimilate," was in substance an attempt to
show that the early Church, to which the Tractarians
referred as the embodiment of pure Christianity, was
in fact already corrupt. The obvious difficulty of such
an argument is to stop at the right point. If the early
fathers, to whom Pusey and his friends appealed, were
already unworthy of confidence, what is to be said of
their predecessors? That was just the line taken by
Hennell. He rejects the supernatural explanation in
the case of the first teachers as well as in the case
of their followers. George Eliot's "chart" already
implied an interest in ecclesiastical history which
might lead to a criticism of the origins as well as
of the later development of the creed. It might be
noticed, too, that she was making excursions into
scientific reading — Mrs. Somerville's *Connexion of the
Physical Sciences,* for example — and would, of course,
be interested in the bearing of geology upon the book
of Genesis. But the purely intellectual aspect of the
question was in a great degree subordinate to other
considerations. She told Mrs. Sibree that she had
been shocked by the union of low morality with strong
religious feeling among the poor, chiefly Methodists,
whom she had been in the habit of visiting. There
were, it seems, specimens there of the "Holy Willie"
type. They held to the Calvinism expressed in his
famous prayer —

'O Thou, wha in the heavens dost dwell,
Wha, as it pleases best Thysel',
Sends ain to heaven and ten to hell,
A' for Thy glory,
And no' for onie guid or ill
They 've done afore Thee !'

and apparently were capable of following his very
defective practice. " I do not feel," said a woman convicted of lying, " that I have grieved the Spirit much."
" Calvinism," George Eliot is reported to have said at
the time, " is Christianity, and that granted, it is a
religion based on pure selfishness." I need not ask
whether Christianity can be identified with Calvinism,
or whether antinomianism or pure egoism be in reality
a logical deduction from Calvinism. Anyhow, it is
clear that she might be led to one conclusion. Since
Mrs. Samuel Evans and the lying old woman held
the same dogmatic creed, it followed that Mrs. Evans'
lovely moral nature could not be the product of the
dogmas. Other reflections tended to the same result.
Robert Hall, she said, had been made unhappy for a
week by reading Miss Edgeworth's *Tales*. In them the
characters led good, useful, and pleasant lives without
reference to the cares and fears of religion. They
were, in fact, model Utilitarians. When George Eliot
was asked in later life what influence had unsettled her
orthodoxy, she replied, " Walter Scott's "! Scott has
generally been credited with a different influence.
His romantic tendency was one of the causes, according
to Newman, the highest authority on the point, which
led to the reaction towards the mediæval Church.
George Eliot sympathised with another, and perhaps
a really deeper, characteristic of his writings. Scott
was a man of sympathies wide enough to do justice to

many different types. He hated the fanaticism of the Covenanters, and speaks of them in his letters as scarcely human except in outward form. Yet he was too good an artist to yield to his antipathies; and in *Old Mortality* and the *Heart of Midlothian* has drawn the most striking pictures of the iron heroism and stern morality of the sect. George Eliot would have taken a similar view of Balfour of Burley and Davie Deans. But, in a wider sense, it is obvious that while Scott sincerely respects religious feelings and sympathises with belief, he shows as little sectarian zeal as Shakespeare. The division between good and bad does not correspond in his pages with the division between any one church and its antagonists. The qualities which he really admires — manliness, patriotism, unflinching loyalty, and purity of life — are to be found equally among Protestants and Catholics, Roundheads and Cavaliers. The wide sympathy which sees good and bad on all sides makes it difficult to accept any version of the doctrine which supposes salvation to be associated with the acceptance of a dogma. That clearly was George Eliot's frame of mind. She would not directly attack her young friend's Evangelicism, but she smiled in the kindest way at the doctrine that there could be no true morality without it. "The great lesson of life," she said, "is tolerance," and a width of sympathy was perhaps her most characteristic quality. Her revolt from orthodox views was therefore unaccompanied by the bitterness which often accompanies the emancipation from the strictness of a sectarian tyranny. She continued to revere her aunt; only she had made up her mind that the beauty of character was in no sense the product of the creed. Nor, on the other hand, had it produced the immorality of coarse hypocrites. Taken literally and seriously, the dogmas might tend to suppress and trammel the emotional nature; but, in point of fact, beautiful souls manage to turn even their creeds to account by an unconscious logical artifice which leaves the dark side out of sight and dwells upon the higher and gentler aspirations embodied.

Her first recognition of a change of creed engendered a passing aggressiveness. A Baptist minister was induced by Miss Franklin to attempt a recovery of the lost sheep. "That young lady," he said, "must have had the devil at her elbow to suggest doubts, for there was not a book that I recommended to her in support of Christian evidences that she had not read." The phrase is a little ambiguous, and may be taken to attribute the books on the evidences to the devil's suggestion. "I have attended the University sermon for forty years," said a well-known Squire Bedell, "and I thank God that I am still a Christian." An unconvincing refutation is apt to be irritating, and for a time George Eliot was stimulated to the combative mood. Her father was a "churchman of the old school." His religious notions partook of those ascribed in the *Mill on the Floss* to Mr. Tulliver and the Dodsons. They, we are told, had the strongest respect for whatever was customary, including an acceptance of the rites of the Established Church; though their "theory of life" had "the very slightest tincture of theology." Mr. Evans was so much annoyed by his daughter's abandonment of churchgoing, that he resolved to give up the house at Coventry and to

take up his abode with his married daughter. George
Eliot proposed to take lodgings at Leamington and
try to support herself by teaching. Friends on both
sides, however, effected a reconciliation. She agreed
to go to church again, and her father was glad to
receive her again upon those terms, and apparently
asked no questions about her opinions, and made no
difficulty as to the employment of her talents which
they were soon to suggest. Some months later she
wrote to Sara Hennell, giving the view to which she
had been brought by further reflection. "When the
soul," she says, "is just liberated from the wretched
giant's bed of dogmas on which it has been racked
and stretched ever since it began to think, there is a
feeling of exultation and strong hope. In that state
of mind we wish to proselytise." We soon find that
we can ourselves "ill afford to part even with the
crutch of superstition," and that the errors which we
took to be a "mere incrustation" have grown into the
living body, "and cannot be wrenched away without
destroying vitality." Intellectual agreement seems to
be unattainable, and "we turn to the *truth of feeling* as
the only universal bond of union." It is quackery to
say to every one, "Swallow my opinions and you shall
be whole." When the proselytising impulse is abandoned, we ask, "Are we to remain aloof from our fellow-
creatures on occasions when we may fully sympathise
with the feelings exercised, although our own have
been melted into another mood? Ought we not on
every opportunity to seek to have our feelings in
harmony, though not in union, with those who are
often richer in the fruits of faith, though not in reason,
than ourselves?" The position is characteristic of her

attitude through life. She shrank with deep repugnance from attacking even what she regarded as superstitions which, in the minds of believers, were interwoven with the highest aspirations. She still insists upon the necessity of free discussion and open avowals of honest belief; but her own temperament demanded the tenderest treatment of other creeds. To her exquisitely sensitive nature, the pain of inflicting pain on others would not have been compensated by any share of the true controversialist's joy in battle. In later years she did not hold that she had deserved blame for the domestic difficulty, but she regretted a collision which might have been avoided by judicious management.

The reconciliation was made in the spring of 1842, and for the next seven years George Eliot lived at Coventry with her father. The friendship with the Brays provided her with congenial society and intellectual sympathy. She made summer expeditions with them to Wales, the Lakes (where she made acquaintance with Miss Martineau), and Scotland. She met Robert Owen at their house, and thought that if his system flourished, it would be in spite of the founder; and some time later Emerson came to see them, and she went with him and the Brays to Stratford-on-Avon. "He is," she says, "the first *man* I have ever seen"; but does not expound the statement, and it does not appear that Emerson had any specific influence upon her mind. Meanwhile, she had been led to her first important piece of literary work. An excursion with the Brays and Hennells was shared by Miss Brabant, daughter of Dr. Brabant of Devizes, and followed by the engagement of Miss Brabant to

Charles Hennell.   Dr. Brabant was a personal friend
of Strauss, and his daughter had undertaken a translation of Strauss's *Life of Jesus*, for which funds were
provided by Joseph Parkes (well known as a Radical
politician) and others.   Before her marriage she gave
up the task, which was transferred to George Eliot in
January 1844.   For the next two years George Eliot's
energies were absorbed in this task.   Translating in
general is not very exhilarating work, nor Strauss's book
specially exhilarating to translate.   Before the book
was finished she was often depressed, and towards the
end thoroughly bored.   She was encouraged by Sara
Hennell when she had ceased to " sit down to Strauss
with any relish," and was longing for proof sheets to
convince her that her " soul-stupefying labour " would
not be thrown away.   She worked, however, in the
most conscientious way, and finally achieved an admirable and workmanlike translation.   Dull as the labour
was, the continual effort at accurate reproduction was
probably of some use to her English style.   Whether
her father knew of her employment, or thought that
her churchgoing made amends for her share in propa-
gating scepticism, is not recorded.   She seems from her
letters to have accepted Strauss's general position,
though now and then she had qualms.   She says,
writes Mrs. Bray in 1846, that " she is Strauss-sick ;
it makes her ill dissecting the beautiful story of the
Crucifixion, and only the sight of the Christ image "
(a statuette after Thorwaldsen in her study) "and
picture made her endure it."   To others the image
might perhaps have suggested rather remonstrance
than encouragement.   The book appeared, without
the translator's name, in June 1846.

Her father's health was now beginning to break, and her time was much occupied for the next three years by her devoted care of him. She did all the nursing herself, and is reported to have done it admirably. In the latter part of the time she found some distraction in beginning a translation of Spinoza's *Tractatus Theologico-Politicus*. Her letters give a few indications of her thoughts upon the outward events of an exciting time. She sympathised warmly with the French Revolution of 1848, and admired Lamartine and Louis Blanc. She shows, however, some misgiving, and is depressed by the contrast between French enthusiasts and their English sympathisers. Englishmen have a much larger proportion of " selfish radicalism and un-satisfied brute sensuality than of perception or desire of justice"; and a revolution here would be simply destructive. A little later she is made melancholy by the tone of the newspapers about Louis Blanc: " The day will come when there will be a temple of white marble, where sweet incense and anthems shall rise to the memory of every man and woman who has had . . . a clear vision of the time when this miserable reign of Mammon shall end." She has, she says, been wrought into fury " by the loathsome fawning, the transparent hypocrisy, the systematic giving as little as possible for as much as possible, that one meets with here at every turn. I feel that society is training men and women for hell." In this high-wrought and pessimistic frame of mind she speaks with remarkable enthusiasm of Rousseau and George Sand. Spite of all that may be said against him, Rousseau's genius has " sent that electric thrill through my intellectual and moral frame which has wakened me to new perceptions, which has

D

made man and nature a fresh world of thought and feeling to me; and this not by teaching me any new belief." The "rushing mighty wind of his inspiration has so quickened my faculties that I have been able to shape more definitely for myself ideas which had previously dwelt as dim *Ahnungen* in my soul." George Sand has a similar power. "It is sufficient for me as a reason for bowing before her in eternal gratitude to that 'great power of God manifested in her' that I cannot read six pages of hers without feeling that it is given to her to delineate human passion and its results, and (I must say, in spite of your judgment) some of the moral instincts and their tendencies, with such truthfulness, such nicety of discrimination, such tragic power, and withal such loving gentle humour, that one might live a century with nothing but one's own dull faculties and not know so much as those six pages will suggest." She adds that she has just acquired a "most delightful" *De Imitatione Christi*, with quaint woodcuts — a book which affected Maggie Tulliver in the same way. "It makes one long to be a saint for a few months. Verily, its piety has its foundations in the depth of the dumb human soul." One may note, too, in passing, her delight in *Sir Charles Grandison*. "The morality," she says, "is perfect — there is nothing for the new lights to correct." During this period she must have been accumulating the experience to be turned to account in *Middlemarch*. It is curious to contrast the tone of that book with the passionate enthusiasm for such prophets of sentimentalism as Richardson, Rousseau, or George Sand. But of this I must speak hereafter.

She was meanwhile soothing her father's last hours

of consciousness by reading the Waverley novels. He died on the 31st May 1849. "What shall I be without him?" she asks. "It will seem as if a part of my moral nature were gone." Soon afterward she joined the Brays in a visit to the continent. They went through France to the North of Italy, and returned by Switzerland, where she remained at Geneva. There she stayed from July till March 1850, recovering strength and spirits after the long strain caused by her father's illness. For the greater part of the time she was living with M. and Mme. D'Albert, to both of whom she became strongly attached. M. D'Albert was a man of artistic tastes, and became Conservateur of the Athénée — the National Gallery of Geneva. He afterwards translated several of George Eliot's novels ; and the friendship lasted till the end of her life. A fortnight after coming to stay with them, George Eliot says that Mme. D'Albert makes a spoilt child of her, and that she already loves M. D'Albert as "if he were father and brother both. It is so delightful to get among people who exhibit no meannesses, no worldlinesses, that one may well be enthusiastic." In fact, she had fortunately fallen into a thoroughly congenial circle; and her characteristic craving for affection had been satisfied by worthy objects. She admired the beauties of Geneva, had a little quiet and refined society, and left Spinoza's *Tractatus* on the shelf. She attended certain lectures of Professor De la Rive on "Experimental Physics," which we will hope were cheering, but otherwise resigned herself to judicious relaxation. She found, in fact, that Geneva was in itself superior to Coventry, though there were some people at Coventry "better than lake, trees, and

mountains." But for them, she would think with a
shudder of returning to England. "It looks to me
like a land of gloom, of *ennui*, of platitude, but in the
midst of all this it is the land of duty and affection;
and the only ardent hope I have for my future life is
to have given to me some woman's duty, some possibility of devoting myself where I may see a daily
result of pure calm blessedness in the life of another."

The phrase is significant. She was now thirty years
old, and her outlook was sufficiently vague. She had
grown to her full intellectual stature. She had read
widely and intelligently; and if she had not devoted
herself to any special line of inquiry, she was becoming
familiar with the world of ideas which were ignored
in the early domestic circle. So far, however, there
is no appearance of any intention to take up original
work. "We fancy," says Mrs. Bray in 1846, that
"she must be writing her novel," — apparently because
she "is looking very brilliant just now." But the
"novel" appears to be merely conjectural, and her
labours upon Strauss had not suggested a possibility
of her taking up an independent part in such inquiries. Her diffidence would suggest rightly or
wrongly that she was not qualified to contribute to
philosophical or critical literature. She was therefore
at a loss to find any channel for the store of intellectual energy already enriched by much experience
and reflection. A poem, written some years later,
suggests a state of mind which may illustrate her
position at this period. She describes a "Minor
Prophet," a gentleman of Puritan descent who has
taken up new ideas with the old dogmatic confidence.
He is a phrenologist and a vegetarian, interested in

"psychical research," and fully expecting a regeneration of the world by the adoption of scientific inventions and the elimination of "faulty human types." She smiles sadly at the prospect, and feels "short-sighted pity" for the coming man who

> " Will not know half the dear imperfect things
> That move my smiles and tears — will never know
> The fine old incongruities that raise
> My friendly laugh ; the innocent conceits
> That, like a needless eyeglass or black patch,
> Give those who wear them harmless happiness ;
> The twists and cracks in our poor earthenware
> That touch me to more conscious fellowship
> (I am not myself the finest Parian)
> With my coevals."

She goes on to explain that she is anything but indifferent to hopes for another future —

> " The earth yields nothing more divine
> Than high prophetic vision — than the seer
> Who, fasting from man's meaner joy, beholds
> The paths of beauteous order and constructs
> A fairer type, to shame our low content.
> But prophecy is like potential sound
> Which turned to music seems a voice sublime
> From out the soul of light, but turns to noise
> In scrannel pipes and makes all ears averse."

She is, she would seem to intimate, distracted between the past and the present; between the old-fashioned Griff and the society of the squires and farmers, narrow and stupid, but somehow picturesque, cordial, and humorous; and the pragmatical tiresome preacher of scientific or quasi-scientific "fads," who is as undeniably right in his aspirations as he is intolerably prosaic and harsh in his judgment of his predecessors. Now Mr. Bray clearly did not stand for the minor prophet. George Eliot was far too loyal to her friends not to be a little blind to their defects; and Bray was a man of real sense and ability. Yet the " minor prophet " was a kind of inferior Bray, and among his disciples and colleagues there were plenty of people who showed the ugly side of scientific arrogance and the readiness to substitute a tune upon " scrannel pipes " for the pathetic if imperfect music of the older creeds. George Eliot desired to sympathise with these leaders of progress, but contempt for the past jarred most painfully upon her feelings, and seemed treasonable to the best human affections. The intensely tender and sensitive nature which prompted her longing for some " woman's mission " made her shrink from too close an alliance with the iconoclasts who would indiscriminately condemn things sacred to her memory.

CHAPTER III

UPON her return from Geneva, George Eliot had gone to the Brays, with whom she stayed for some months. A turning-point in her life was now to occur. The *Westminster Review*, started originally by the Benthamites in their most hopeful days, was in its normal state of insufficient circulation. J. S. Mill had given it up when the decline of the "philosophical radicals" made the management of their organ a thankless task. Since his day it had been in the hands of Mr. Hickson. It was now to be transferred to Mr. Chapman, who hoped to make it an adequate organ for the best liberal thought of the day. He paid a visit to the Brays in October 1850 with Robert William Mackay, an amiable and accomplished man whose chief work, *The Progress of the Intellect*, had just appeared. George Eliot wrote a sympathetic review of this book for the *Westminster Review*. Her article was in the number for January 1851, and was the first writing in which she attempted anything more ambitious than translation. Mackay's aim, as she defines it, was to show that "divine revelation" is not to be found exclusively in the records of any one nation, "but is co-extensive with the history of human development." A phrase about the "inexorable law of consequences" shows that she was still a disciple of Bray, who praises her for illustrating that "law" in her novels. She seems, too, to have accepted the phrenology of Combe and Bray, as is shown by occasional references to the "anterior lobes" of such great men as Dickens and Professor Owen, whom she was presently to see. Chapman finally bought the *Westminster*, and arranged that George Eliot should become assistant editor. She took up her duties in September 1851, and boarded with the Chapmans at their house in the Strand. Her wide knowledge of foreign and English literature, her industry and willingness to perform any kind of drudgery, were admirable qualifications for the post. It might be doubted whether a young lady who had hitherto lived only in the provinces, and had had no concern in periodical literature, would possess an instinct for the qualities which secure popular success. That, however, would be mainly a question for the Editor-in-chief, and the *Westminster* endeavoured to make its way by enlisting contributors already distinguished or soon to win distinction. The list of persons who were more or less interested in the undertaking is remarkable, and in one way or other George Eliot saw something of most of the writers who have left their mark upon the time. Some of the lights have paled. She is introduced to the daughter of the *Religion of the Universe*, and perhaps few readers will be able to say offhand that the phrase means the religion of Mr. Robert Fellowes. But in many cases we regret that her letters, written hastily in the intervals of continuous labour, give us only tantalising glimpses. The philosophical radicals had ceased to be efficient contributors. J. S. Mill, whose

position had been established by the *Logic* and the
Political Economy, was at this time much of a recluse.
He was, however, "propitiated" by Grote, who was
"very friendly," and he contributed one article (upon
Whewell's *Moral Philosophy*) of which the sub-editor
did not think highly. Mill's early friend, William
Ellis, of whose "apostolical labour" in trying to get
Political Economy taught in primary schools he spoke
enthusiastically, was personally kind, but does not
appear to have contributed. Carlyle, who had just
published *The Life of Sterling*, and beginning to plunge
into *Frederick*, was invited to denounce the peerage.
"Insinuating letters," offering "three other most
glorious subjects," failed to bring him down, but he
called and strongly, though fruitlessly, recommended
"Browning the poet." With Froude, then just becoming a disciple of the prophet, she was more fortunate. She had greatly admired the *Nemesis of Faith,*
and written a notice of it for the *Coventry Herald.* A
personal acquaintance had followed; and but for his
marriage at the time, Froude would have joined the
Brays in their trip with her to Geneva. He now
contributed a striking article upon the Book of Job,
and afterwards wrote upon Spinoza. The number in
which the "Job" appeared included contributions
from Theodore Parker and Harriet Martineau. Miss
Martineau attracted her by kindness and cordiality,
and was an effective contributor. To James Martineau
there are admiring references, though he generally
wrote in other organs. Francis Newman, whom
she had already called "our blessed St. Francis";
W. R. Greg, whose *Creed of Christendom* had produced
a marked effect; W. J. Fox, the veteran radical

author and orator; and W. E. Forster, who wrote
an article greatly approved by her upon American
Slavery, are other names incidentally mentioned.
Mazzini wrote an article, pronounced by Greg to be
"sad stuff." The most important contributor, however, appears to have been Mr. Herbert Spencer. His
article upon the "Universal Postulate" made a special
impression. He had just brought out his *Social Statics*,
pronounced, as she had heard, by G. H. Lewes to be
the "best book on the subject." They rapidly became
friends, and she declares him to be "a good, delightful
creature." She "always feels better for being with
him." By Mr. Herbert Spencer she was introduced
towards the end of 1851 to George Henry Lewes, of
whom more must be said directly.

Meanwhile it may be remarked that she was thus
becoming more or less familiar with nearly all the
eminent writers who, in one sense or other, were on
the side of intellectual advance. They differed widely
enough from each other, and there could hardly be a
more fundamental contrast than that between Carlyle
and Mr. Herbert Spencer. It was as well that she
should learn that the Brays and Hennells, however
excellent in their way, did not represent the only line
of thought. She had, indeed, read too widely to be
kept within the prison house of a single sect. One
point may be noticed in passing, as it had a marked
influence upon her later views. The philosophy of
Comte was at this time attracting notice in England.
Mill had been for a time a warm personal disciple, and
had spoken of him with great respect in the *Logic;* Miss
Martineau was compiling an abridgment of his work;
and G. H. Lewes had written as an adherent of his

doctrine.   George Eliot was interested ; and in later
life drew nearer to the Positivist than to any other
school.   Her editorial work seems to have been absorbing and often dispiriting.   It was too much like
flogging a dead horse.   The public declined to care
for the admirable articles addressed to them, and
showed no very keen hankering for sound philosophy.
She had to plod through much ponderous manuscript
on arid topics.   Her hands, she complains, are "hot
and tremulous," while there is a "great dreary article"
by her side asking for reading and abridgment.   One
day she has to read a review article upon taxation, to
collate it with newspaper articles, and consider all that
J. S. Mill says on the subject.   Then Mr. Chapman
produces a thick German volume, of which she is to
read enough to form an opinion.   Mr. Lewes calls, and
"of course sits talking till the second bell rings," and
at 11 P.M. she is still puzzling over taxation.   Letters
and callers and meetings of Associations distract her,
and she is glad to fly for occasional relief to her friends
at Coventry.   In addition to her regular work she is
translating Ludwig Feuerbach's *Essence of Christianity*,
which appeared as by "Marian Evans" (the only time
her real name was used) in July 1854.   Feuerbach
had developed Hegelianism into naturalism, and the
translation apparently implies an extension of George
Eliot's anti-theological tendencies.   Another book by
her on the *Idea of a Future Life* was advertised, but
never appeared.   She complains of headaches and
rheumatism ; and one is not surprised that by the end
of 1853 she is becoming tired of it, and is giving notice
of resignation to Mr. Chapman.   She was living alone
in lodgings, snatching brief holidays to be spent with

the Brays, and, we may guess, feeling the want of the domestic circle, which, even when not intellectually sympathetic, had satisfied her craving for affection.

George Henry Lewes, born in 1817, if not the profoundest reasoner, was certainly one of the most brilliant of the literary celebrities of the time. He was the grandson of a second-rate actor, and had had a very desultory education. The dates and facts seem to be rather confused. He had, it is said, passed through several schools, had then been a clerk in a merchant's office, and for some time a medical student; he had spent some years in France and Germany, and almost forgotten the use of his mother tongue. On returning to England he had for a time gone upon the stage; at the age of twenty he had given lectures upon philosophy at the chapel of W. J. Fox; and he had finally settled down to write books and articles on the most various topics. He had written a play and a couple of novels, one of which, *Rose, Blanche, and Violet*, made something of a mark. He had written articles upon French and German philosophy and literature; discoursed upon the Greek, Spanish, and Italian drama; and criticised Browning, Tennyson, and Macaulay. His *Biographical History of Philosophy*, which appeared in 1845 and 1846, showed that in spite of all distracting interests he thought himself qualified to expound ultimate truths. Learned professors who, like Sir William Hamilton, had spent lives upon abstruse metaphysical treatises, might despise the audacity of the young man who entered the arena with so slender an apparatus of learning. The brightness and vivacity of the book, however, and the happy introduction of the biographical element, roused the interest of ordinary readers, and perhaps persuaded some of them that much of the mystery in which the more ponderous philosophers wrapped themselves could be dispelled by a little common sense. The preface, indeed, announced that "philosophy" had had its day, and was to be superseded by Comte's Positivism. Lewes afterwards wrote the *Life of Goethe*, which though ardent Goethe worshippers may pronounce it to show a want of sympathy for some aspects of the hero, is singularly interesting and well written, and deserved the success which has made it a standard work in biography. He afterwards took to physiology, and after producing some popular books, approved, it is said, by "scientific bigwigs," proceeded to show the philosophical bearing of his studies in his *Problems of Life and Mind*. This was left as a fragment at his death. I need only say here that whatever their value, his later writings show the old alertness and keenness of intellect and his continued interest in the philosophical disquisitions to which, spite of all distractions, he was constantly recurring.

At this time Lewes was literary editor of the *Leader*, a weekly paper representing the same tendencies as the *Westminster*. He was publishing a series of articles upon Comte, to whom he had been personally introduced by J. S. Mill. He was what is generally called a Bohemian, though always with a serious ambition. He could converse ably upon all such matters as interested literary and journalistic circles in London, and his wide knowledge of continental writers gave him an authority in some matters not shared by many English contemporaries. He was a brilliant talker, fully able to turn his knowledge to

account. His conversation abounded in lively anecdotes, told with infinite zest; he was thoroughly
genial, and ready at good-humoured repartee; and he
was not hampered by any excessive reverence for conventional proprieties. He was of slight figure, and,
according to Douglas Jerrold, the "ugliest man in
London." It would be presumptuous to express any
opinion upon the justice of so sweeping an observation.
But if not beautiful, he was a man to forget, and to
induce companions to forget, any such defects. He
had bright eyes and a fine brow, and the whole face
and bearing was full of intelligence. A social gathering must have consisted of very ponderous interests
if it could not be stirred into animation by a man with
so much more quicksilver in his composition than falls
to the lot of the average Briton. Nobody, one might
guess, was more likely to dazzle the grave young
lady, profoundly interested in philosophy, and anxious
to get the newest lights in speculation, than this
daring and brilliant writer, who knew all that was
being done in France and Germany, and could talk
with equal confidence upon Comte and Hegel, or upon
the last new play or oratorio in London. She was
apparently rather repelled by his levity at first; but
after a time says that he has "quite won her liking
in spite of herself." He has had a good deal of her
"vituperation"; but, "like a few other people in the
world, he is much better than he seems — a man of
heart and conscience, wearing a mask of flippancy."

Lewes had married in 1840. He was at this time
living in the same house with Thornton Hunt, who
had edited the *Leader* in co-operation with him. Mrs.
Lewes preferred Thornton Hunt to her husband,

to whom she had already borne children. Though
Lewes's views of the marriage tie were anything but
strict, this had led some two years previously to a
break-up of his family. A legal divorce was impossible; but George Eliot held that the circumstances
justified her in forming a union with Lewes, which
she considered as equivalent to a legitimate marriage.
I have not, and I suppose that no one now has, the
knowledge which would be necessary for giving an
opinion as to the proper distribution of praise and
blame among the various parties concerned, nor shall
I argue the ethical question raised by George Eliot's
conduct. It may be a pretty problem for casuists
whether the breach of an assumed moral law is aggra-
vated or extenuated by the offender's honest conviction
that the law is not moral at all. George Eliot at any
rate emphatically took that position. She had long
protested against the absolute indissolubility of marriage. She thought, we are told, that the system
worked badly, because wives were less anxious to please
their husbands when their position was "invulnerable."
She held, with Milton, that so close a tie between
persons not united in soul was intolerable. " All self-
sacrifice is good," she had said upon reading *Jane Eyre*
in 1848, " but one would like it to be in a somewhat
nobler cause than that of a diabolical law which chains
a man body and soul to a putrefying carcase." Mrs.
Lewes was not so bad as Mrs. Rochester, but the
hardship was sufficient to justify an exception to the
ordinary rule. Writing a few months after the union,
she says that she cannot understand how any un-
worldly unsuperstitious person, who is sufficiently
" acquainted with the realities of life," can pronounce

her relation to Lewes " immoral." Nothing in her
life, she declares, has been more " profoundly serious,"
which means, it seems, that she does not approve
" light and easily broken ties." In her writings,
indeed, her tendency is to insist upon the sanctity of
the traditional bonds, which, whatever their origin,
are essential to social welfare, and so far she agrees on
this, as on many points, with her friends the Positivists.
Comte, though he admired the Catholic doctrine of
the indissolubility of marriage, discovered the necessity
for making an exception which happened to cover his
own case. George Eliot, it seems, who had never
accepted the strictest doctrine, was more consistent.
No one can deny that the relation to Lewes was
" serious " enough in her sense. It lasted through
their common lives, and their devotion to each other
was unlimited, and appears only to have strengthened
with time. She never misses an opportunity of ex-
pressing her affection for her " husband," or her gratitude for the blessings due to his devotion. Lewes
expressed his feeling with equal emphasis. In a
journal of 1859 he speaks of a walk with Mr. Herbert
Spencer. Mr. Spencer's friendship had been the
brightest ray in a very dreary " wasted period of my
life "; it had roused him from indifference to fresh
intellectual interest; but, he adds, " I owe Spencer
another and a deeper debt. It was through him
that I learned to know Marian — to know her was to
love her — and since then my life has been a new
birth. To her I owe all my prosperity and all my
happiness. God bless her ! " Lewes, like other men
of his buoyant temperament, was well enough satisfied
with himself ; but his vanity was made inoffensive by

his generosity. He recognised all talent gladly; and the recognition in the case of George Eliot rose to enthusiastic devotion. He looked up to her as in her own field an entirely superior being, in the front rank of contemporary genius. Their house became a temple of a domestic worship, in which he was content to be the high priest of the presiding deity. He stood as much as possible between her and all the worries of the outside world. He transacted her business, wrote her letters, kept her from the knowledge of unpleasant criticism, read all her books with her as they were composed, made suggestions and occasional criticisms; but, above all, encouraged her by hearty and sincere praise during the fits of depression to which she was constitutionally liable. She gave him the manuscripts of her books with inscriptions recording her gratitude, and the inscription in *Romola* may sum up her permanent sentiment: " To the Husband, whose perfect love has been the best source of her insight and strength, this manuscript is given by his devoted wife, the writer."

The Leweses left England together in July 1854 and went to Weimar, where he worked upon the *Life of Goethe*. In November they went to Berlin, and returned to England in March 1855. They saw a good many distinguished Germans, only one of whom " seemed conscious of his countrymen's deficiencies." They were, however, kindly received; and George Eliot's intellectual horizon was no doubt widened by intercourse with Rauch the sculptor, Liszt the musician, Liebig the chemist, Varnhagen von Ense, and others well known in various departments. She worked at a translation of Spinoza's *Ethics*, which

E

was never published, though much of it seems to have been completed. On reaching England they settled for a time at Richmond, and had to take seriously to writing. Lewes had to support his wife's children, and both had to depend upon their pens. Lewes was bringing out his *Life of Goethe*. George Eliot continued her labours upon Spinoza, and contributed articles to the *Westminster* and other periodicals. She wrote upon Heine, Young of the *Night Thoughts*, Margaret Fuller, and Mary Wollstonecraft, and upon Dr. Cumming, who in those days was interpreting the Apocalypse and thrilling simple readers by a prospect of the approaching battle of Armageddon. Her remarks upon Cumming — rather small game, it must be admitted, for such an adversary — had one result. They convinced Lewes that she possessed not only great talent, but true genius. In 1856 the Leweses made some stay at Ilfracombe and Tenby, where Lewes was seeking materials for his *Seaside Studies*. Upon their return to Richmond in September, George Eliot at last took up the work by which she was to become famous.

CHAPTER IV

SCENES OF CLERICAL LIFE

HITHERTO George Eliot, who was now thirty-six, had confined herself to comparatively humble work. She was at home in the upper sphere of philosophy and the historical criticism of religion; but she was content to be an expositor of the views of independent thinkers. She had spent years of toil upon translating Strauss, Feuerbach, and Spinoza; and was fully competent to be in intellectual communion with her friends Charles Bray and Mr. Herbert Spencer. It does not appear, however, that she ever aspired to make original contributions to speculative thought. The effect of her philosophical studies upon her imaginative work was very marked; but she was not to be the first example of a female metaphysician of high rank. She was only to be the first female novelist whose inspiration came in a great degree from a philosophical creed. I have already spoken of the apparently slow development of the purely artistic impulse. Most women at the present day begin, I believe, to write novels in their teens. Miss Burney made herself famous at the age of twenty-five by *Evelina*, written some years previously. Miss Brontë had already finished her brilliant career before George Eliot had begun to write. The most famous of her predecessors, Miss

Austen, had written stories in her childhood, though her first novel, *Sense and Sensibility*, did not appear till she was thirty-five. Miss Edgeworth published her first novel, *Castle Rackrent,* at the age of thirty-three; and Miss Ferrier her *Marriage* at the age of thirty-five. Mrs. Gaskell's (George Eliot's senior by ten years) first novel, *Mary Barton*, appeared when the author was thirty-eight. These precedents may perhaps suggest that women who have the gift have been often kept back by the feminine virtue of diffidence. Of that virtue, if it be a virtue, George Eliot undoubtedly possessed a large share, and the circumstances of her youth fostered the tendency. Her reverence for her intellectual guides, who were not much given to novel-reading and writing, would act in the same direction. Mr. Herbert Spencer's philosophy may be admirable in its own sphere, but is not of itself likely to stimulate an interest in purely imaginative work. It almost seems as if George Eliot would never have written a novel at all had it not been for the quick perception of Lewes. In their circumstances, too, there were sound utilitarian reasons for trying an experiment in the direction of the most profitable variety of literature.

George Eliot indeed had always cherished a " vague dream " that some time or other she might write a novel. She had as yet got no further than an " introductory chapter " descriptive of life in a Staffordshire village and the neighbouring farmhouses. The dream had died away. She became despondent of success in that, as in other undertakings. She thought that, though she could describe, she had no dramatic or constructive power. She happened, however, to have

the old fragment with her in Germany, and read it to
Lewes one evening at Berlin.   He shared her doubts
as to the dramatic power; but the ability shown in
her other articles led him to think the experiment of
novel-writing worth trying.   One day, in a dreamy
mood, she fancied herself writing a story to be called
" The Sad Fortunes of the Rev. Amos Barton."   Lewes
was struck by the title, and encouraged her to make
a start.   " You have wit, description, and philosophy,"
he would say; "those go a good way towards the
production of a novel."   On 22nd September she at
last began to write.   She showed the first part to
Lewes, suggesting that it might open a series of
sketches drawn from her observations of the clergy.
The scene at Cross Farm convinced him that she could
write good dialogue.   It was still to be seen whether
she had a command of pathos.   This was settled by a
chapter describing the last illness of Mrs. Barton.
They both "cried over it," and Lewes kissed her,
saying, " I think your pathos is better than your
fun."   Thus encouraged, she finished the story on the
5th of November, and next day Lewes sent the ms.
with a note to John Blackwood.   Lewes stated that
the story, intended for the first of a series, had been
written by a friend whose powers he had doubted.
The doubts had been changed by the reading into " very
high admiration."   " Such humour, pathos, vivid presentation, and nice observation," he thought, " had
not been exhibited in this style since the *Vicar of
Wakefield.*"   Blackwood answered, saying that the
story " would do," though making some criticisms,
and adding that till he had seen more of the proposed
series he could not make " any decided proposition for

the publication of the Tales " in the *Magazine*. The
rather guarded approval called forth a stronger eulogy
from Lewes, declaring that the story showed the rarest
of all faculties — " dramatic ventriloquism." A pub-
lisher can hardly be expected to praise too enthusiastically the wares for which he is bargaining. As
Blackwood put it undeniably, "criticism would assume
a much soberer tone were critics compelled seriously
to act whenever they expressed an opinion." He
showed his genuine opinion by accepting the story
at once, and waiving his objection to taking it without
seeing its successors. The confidence of Lewes's friend,
which had been shaken, was greatly restored by this
letter. " He " was afraid, said Lewes, of failure, and
" by failure would understand that which I suspect
most writers would be apt to consider as success — so
high is his ambition. I tell you this," added Lewes,
" that you may understand the sort of shy, shrinking,
ambitious nature you have to deal with." The first
part of the story accordingly appeared in *Blackwood's
Magazine* in January 1857 ; and Blackwood sent fifty
guineas and some very cordial praises in return. " Mr.
Gilfil's Love Story " and " Janet's Repentance " appeared in the *Magazine* in the following months; and
these appeared together as *Scenes of Clerical Life* at the
beginning of 1858. The name " George Eliot," under
which these and all her later works appeared, was
assumed, it appears, because Lewes's name was George,
and " Eliot " was " a good mouth-filling, easily pronounced word." She had intended to continue the
series ; but Blackwood's " want of sympathy with the
first part " of " Janet's Repentance " had annoyed her,
though he came round to admiration of the third

part. She wound up the book, therefore, and in October began a more elaborate work.

The *Scenes of Clerical Life* soon attracted notice, though the quiet tone was hardly calculated to produce an instantaneous success of the startling kind. Copies of the collective edition were sent to Froude, Dickens, Thackeray, Tennyson, Ruskin, Faraday, Helps, Albert Smith, and Mrs. Carlyle. Mrs. Carlyle wrote warmly, and declared in Carlylean phrase that "it was a *human* book, written out of the heart of a man, not merely out of the brain of an author, full of tenderness and pathos, without a scrap of sentimentality, of sense without dogmatism, of earnestness without twaddle — a book that makes one *feel friends* at once and for always with the man or woman who wrote it." Carlyle, she added, had promised for once to break his rule of never reading novels when he should emerge from *Frederick.* Froude was also cordial, but the most enthusiastic praise came from Dickens. He had never, he declared, seen the like of the "exquisite truth and delicacy both of the humour and pathos of these stories." Upon another point Dickens showed a keener insight than other writers. In spite of the assumed name, he thought that the author must be a woman. If not, "no man ever before had the art of making himself so like a woman since the world began." Mrs. Carlyle suggested a more complex hypothesis, such as is often put forward in the regions of the "higher criticism." The author might be first cousin to a clergyman, with a wife from whom he had got the "beautiful feminine touches." Thackeray, it was reported, though he "spoke highly" of the book, thought that the author was a man, which, if true, gives a superfluous proof that even the finest critics are fallible. Meanwhile, it seems that certain touches in the book had convinced George Eliot's old neighbours that the author came from their district. The Scenes, as she admitted soon afterwards, contained "portraits," a mistake which should not occur again, and was due to the fact that her "hand was not well in." The plots, too, were more or less reproductions of remembered incidents. Milly Barton, we are told, is the wife of a Mr. Gwyther, curate of Chilvers-Coton. He died when George Eliot was sixteen, and was a friend of Mrs. Robert Evans, who appears in the story as Mrs. Hacket. A persecution of a clergyman, like that upon which *Janet's Repentance* turns, really took place, though she filled in details from imagination. *Mr. Gilfil's Love Story* was a more interesting application of the same method. Sir Christopher and Lady Cheverel represent Sir Roger and Lady Newdigate. The Newdigates had taken charge of a girl called Sally Shilton, daughter of a collier on the property, who had given promise of musical talent. They had her trained as a singer; and when ill-health forced her to give up the attempt, they continued their protection. She married a Mr. Ebdell, vicar of Chilvers-Coton (the "Shepperton" of the story), in 1801, and died twenty-two years later. Sir Roger's heir, Charles Parker, died suddenly, when Sally was a little over twenty, in 1795. George Eliot, who must have learned the facts from family tradition, converted Sally Shilton into Caterina Sarti, by way of explaining her musical talent as a case of "heredity," and then invented the love affair with Captain Wybrow, who takes the place of Charles Parker.

Thus a very touching and consistent love story is
based upon a true history, though Charles Parker in
his new character has to be guilty of a thoughtless
flirtation in which he never indulged, and Sally Shilton
is sentenced to a shorter life than she really enjoyed.
The representatives of the Newdigate family seem to
have regarded this adaptation of their family history
as rather impertinent; and though Sir Christopher is
admitted to be an admirable portrait of Sir Roger, we
are assured that other persons concerned were better
than their representatives. As George Eliot must
have learned the story from common talk, and given a
more distinct colouring to it from her familiarity with
Arbury House and the family portraits, and then
modified the characters so as to make them work out
the story effectively, the deviation from literal truth
will not scandalise those who have not the honour to
be Newdigates. To them the interest lies in the skill
with which these childish recollections have been converted into one of the most charming of stories. The
critic of this first book might perhaps be content with
saying ditto to Lewes, Mrs. Carlyle, and Dickens. At
most he might be inclined to make a few deductions
from the superlatives which are natural, or, one would
rather say, commendable in an enthusiastic recognition
of a new writer of genius. Some defects perhaps show
that the writer had not yet acquired a full command
of her art. In writing to Blackwood, she says that
her " scientific illustrations [in *Amos Barton*] must be
a fault, since they seem to have obtruded themselves
disagreeably on one of my readers." She declares her
innocence of any but a superficial knowledge of science.
The one reader showed some acuteness, for the

scientific allusions are not yet so prominent as they came to be in her later style. In the society of Lewes and his friends a scientific allusion, which might alarm the average reader of a magazine, would no doubt pass for commonplace. George Eliot's environment was always so scientific and philosophical that it would have been difficult to be quite free from the taint. The weakness does not imply affectation, and should be taken as an implied, if undeserved, compliment to the reader's intelligence. Blackwood seems to have been vexed by a different indication of defective skill in this story. He did not like the " wind up," and thought that there was " too minute a specification " of the children who gather round Milly Barton's deathbed, and of other persons not previously introduced. I confess that, as the story now stands, I see no force in this criticism; but it may, I think, be said that it marks a slight awkwardness. George Eliot, it would seem, wanted to draw a portrait of the rustic society, and she wanders a little from the main situation in search of characteristic touches. The description of the clerical dinner party seems to be dragged in merely for the purpose of describing different types of clergymen; and here, and in the rather irrelevant Mr. Farquhar, we probably have some of the undesirable portraits from life. If this be true, and I only pretend to speak for myself, the weakness entirely disappears in *Mr. Gilfil's Love Story*. That appears to be almost faultless, and as admirable a specimen of the literary genus to which it belongs as was ever written. *Janet's Repentance* is to me less pleasing for a different reason. The coarse attorney, Dempster, to whom Janet is made a victim, is undoubtedly drawn with

great vigour, and is perhaps one of the characters which
convinced readers that his creator must be of his own
sex.   Lady novelists are not generally familiar with
such blackguards.   Janet, however, is so charming as
to make her subjection to the snuffy, brandy-smelling,
wife-beating bully a little too repulsive; and, moreover, I fancy that a really sharp lawyer would have
found some less clumsy methods of insulting the
evangelical clergyman.   With all her keenness of
observation, George Eliot seems to be getting a little
beyond her tether when she enters the bar of the " Red
Lion."

It is, however, needless to insist upon trifling shortcomings, except as they may indicate limitations to be
displayed hereafter.   The stories have a very definite,
and, in spite of certain prejudices suggested by the
word, a very legitimate moral.   Amos Barton, she
admits, is an extremely commonplace person — so
commonplace, indeed, as Blackwood put it, that the
" asinine stupidity of his conduct about the Countess "
disposes one " to kick him."   Commonplace people,
she observes, have consciences and " sublime prompt-
ings to do the painful right"; they have their unspoken
sorrows and their sacred joys; their hearts have perhaps " gone out towards their firstborn, and they have
mourned over the irreclaimable dead. . . . Depend
upon it, you would gain unspeakably if you would
learn with me to see some of the poetry and the
pathos, the tragedy and comedy, lying in the experience of a human soul that looks out through dull
grey eyes and that speaks in a voice of quite ordinary
tones."   In a letter written after her next book, she
gives her theory : " If art does not enlarge men's

sympathies, it does nothing morally. . . . The only effect I ardently long to produce by my writings is that those who read them should be better able to *imagine* and to *feel* the pains and the joys of those who differ from themselves in everything but the broad fact of being struggling, erring human creatures." This is apparently meant to meet some remonstrance against her recognition of good qualities in characters regarded by her freethinking friends as embodiments of superstitious bigotry. The desire to rouse sympathy for figures who at first sight repel the more cultivated and intelligent is the motive of these stories. Amos Barton, who represents sheer crass stupidity, and Mr. Gilfil, who, to outward appearance, is the old high-and-dry parson, respected by his "bucolic parishioners" for his general shrewdness and special knowledge of shorthorns, and by the squires for his youthful performances in the hunting field, and Mr. Tryan, to whom the evangelicism of Wilberforce and Newton represents the most exalted form of religion, have all had their romances, indicative of true and tender natures beneath the superficial crust of old-fashioned oddities. It is the especial function of the genuine humorist to make such revelations. Sir Roger de Coverley and Parson Adams and Uncle Toby and Dominie Sampson and Colonel Newcome have this much in common that the lovable in them is brought into relief by the superficial oddities; and George Eliot is only following with more consciousness the path which had been indicated by many predecessors of genius. One of whom she always spoke with marked affection was Goldsmith. I remember (it is one of my few reminiscences) to have heard her speaking with enthusiasm of the *Vicar of Wakefield*, and, if my memory be correct, contrasting it with *Paul et Virginie*, much to the advantage of the British author. The Vicar, she held, represented the most wholesome vein in the sentimentalism of the period. I dislike attempts to class literary masterpieces "in order of merit," and I need not here ask what are the qualities to which Goldsmith's inimitable work owes its lasting charm. I think in any case that there is something characteristic in George Eliot's admiration of a book in which the pathos is made effective by a combination of the tenderest feeling with the most exquisite literary tact; and in which we can indulge "great dispositions to cry" without the sense that the crying would have an absurd side. The vicar, however, differs from George Eliot's clergy in this respect (as in many others) that he lives in an idyllic world. Wakefield has, I believe, been identified with some actual locality; but I fancy that it is really in some Arcadia, not to be approached by any boat or railway; and Shepperton, on the contrary, is clearly Chilvers-Coton in Warwickshire, and the inhabitants were but modifications of real people. Miss Mitford's *Village*, which made her reputation in the year of George Eliot's birth, is a description of Three Mile Cross in Berkshire; and Mrs. Gaskell's *Cranford*, which was contributed in 1851 to Dickens's *Household Words*, describes the little town of Knutsford. Both of them are very charming in widely different ways; and in them, as, of course, in Miss Austen, George Eliot had precedents for her choice of a subject. What is characteristic is the tone of feeling and the power of the execution. Dickens's appreciation is the more

creditable to him because the work is conspicuous by
its freedom from his besetting faults. The humour
is perfectly unforced, and shows the comic side of
prosaic commonplace without a touch of grotesque
extravagance, and the pathos is made to tell by
scrupulous self-restraint. Milly Barton dies in the
presence of her husband and children, and we are
never crossed by the thought which disturbs so many
deathbeds in fiction, that she is somehow conscious of
an audience applauding her excellence in the part.
The situations are simple, and the effect is produced
by what we can recognise as the natural development
of the characters involved. And this is the indication
of a profoundly reflective intellect, which contemplates
the little dramas performed by commonplace people
as parts of the wider tragi-comedy of human life; and
the village communities, their thoughts and customs,
as subordinate elements in the great " social organism."
The reflections suggested by Caterina's troubles may
illustrate the remark : " When this poor little heart
was being bruised with a weight too heavy for it,
Nature was holding on her calm inexorable way, in
unmoved and terrible beauty. The stars were rushing in their eternal courses ; the tides swelled to the
level of the last expectant weed ; the sun was making
brilliant day to the busy nations on the other side of
the swift earth. The stream of human thought was
hurrying and broadening onward. The astronomer
was at his telescope ; the great ships were labouring
over the waves ; the toiling eagerness of commerce,
the fierce spirit of revolution, were only ebbing in
brief rest; and sleepless statesmen were dreading the
possible crisis of the morrow. What were our little

Tina and her trouble in this mighty torrent, rushing from one awful unknown to another ? Lighter than the smallest centre of quivering life in the water-drop, hidden and uncared for as the pulse of anguish in the breast of the tiniest bird that has fluttered down to its nest with the long-sought food, and has found the nest empty and torn."

This may recall the famous passage in Carlyle's *French Revolution*, speaking of the fall of the Bastille. It may be that a too frequent and explicit suggestion of such reflections would become tiresome. That criticism cannot, I think, be applied to anything in the *Scenes of Clerical Life*. It is the constant, though not obtrusive, suggestion of the depths below the surface of trivial life which gives an impressive dignity to the work; and, in any case, marks one most distinctive characteristic of George Eliot's genius.

CHAPTER V

ADAM BEDE

THE diffidence from which George Eliot suffered happily took the form of prompting to conscientious workmanship. As Lewes said, she was "ambitious" as well as "shy." That she aimed at so high a mark showed a consciousness of great powers, but not an equal confidence that they could be brought to bear upon the task. A genuine success could only be reached by a strenuous application on a well-considered scheme. The little discouragement of Blackwood's inadequate appreciation of *Janet's Repentance* only induced her to take a larger canvas, which would give room for a fuller manifestation of her genius. She finished *Janet's Repentance* on 9th October 1857, and began *Adam Bede* on 22nd October. She completed the first volume by the following March; wrote the second during a following tour in Germany; and after returning to England at the beginning of September, completed the third volume on 16th November. It was published in the beginning of 1858. When recording these dates in her journal she gives also an interesting account of the genesis of the book. It was suggested by an anecdote which she had heard from an aunt, the Methodist preacher, Mrs. Samuel Evans. Mrs. Evans, she says, was a

" very small, black-eyed woman, who in the days of her strength could not rest without exhorting and remonstrating in season and out of season." She had become much gentler when, at the age of about sixty, she visited Griff and made the acquaintance of her niece. She was very " loving and kind "; and the niece, then under twenty, given to strict reticence about her " inward life," was encouraged to confide in her aunt. This, as already quoted, shows the affectionate relationship which sprang up. They only met twice afterwards, and Mrs. Evans died in 1849. The anecdote which Mrs. Evans had told was of a girl who was hanged for child-murder. Mrs. Evans had passed a night in prayer with her and induced her to make a confession. She afterwards accompanied the criminal in the cart to the place of execution. George Eliot had been deeply affected by this account, and while writing her first story spoke of it to Lewes. He observed, with his keen eye to business, that the prison scene would make an effective incident in a story. The novel was accordingly worked out with a view to this climax. Mrs. Evans was transformed into Dinah Morris, though materially altered in the process. The child-murder implies the seducer, Arthur Donnithorne, and the true lover, Adam Bede. For Adam Bede, she took her father as in some degree the model, though again carefully avoiding direct portraiture. These points established, the general situation is defined, and the development follows simply and naturally. Lewes was responsible for two important points. He was convinced by the first three chapters that Dinah Morris would be the centre of interest for readers. She had there been introduced as preaching

F

and receiving an offer of marriage from Seth Bede.
He inferred that she should be the "principal figure
at the last"; and the remainder of the story was
written with this end "constantly in view." Lewes's
other remark was that Adam Bede was becoming too
passive. He ought to be brought into more direct
collision with Arthur Donnithorne. George Eliot was
impressed by this suggestion; and one night, while
listening to "William Tell" at the Munich Opera, the
fight between the two lovers came upon her as a
"necessity." An account of the way in which a work
of genius has been created is always interesting; and
in this case, I think that it helps to explain some
important characteristics of the story.

Adam Bede, whatever else may be said of it, placed
the author in the first rank of the "Victorian"
novelists. Some of us can still look back with fondness to the middle of the last century, and recall the
period which seems — to our old-fashioned tastes at
least — to have been a flowering time of genius. Within
a few years on either side of 1850 many great lights
of literature arose or culminated. By *David Copper-
field*, which appeared in 1850, Dickens's popular empire,
one may say, was finally established; and if his best
work was done, his admirers steadily increased in
number. Thackeray's *Vanity Fair, Pendennis, Esmond,*
and *The Newcomes* came out between 1847 and 1855.
Miss Brontë's short and most brilliant apparition lasted
from 1847 to 1853. The versatile Bulwer was opening a new and popular vein by *The Caxtons* and *My
Novel* in 1850 and 1853, preaching sound domestic
morality and omitting the True and the Beautiful.
All Charles Kingsley's really powerful works of fiction

— *Alton Locke*, *Yeast*, *Hypatia*, and *Westward Ho !* —
appeared between 1850 and 1855.   Mrs. Gaskell had
first made a mark by *Mary Barton* in 1848, which was
followed by *Cranford* and *North and South*, the last in
1855.   Trollope, after some failures, was beginning to
set forth the humours of Barsetshire by the *Warden* in
1855; and Charles Reade became a popular novelist
by *Christie Johnstone* in 1853, and *Never too late to Mend*
in 1856.   In 1855, I may add, Mr. George Meredith's
Shaving of Shagpat was praised and reviewed by George
Eliot; but the author had long to wait for a general
recognition of his genius.   Anyhow, an ample and
attractive feast was provided for those who had the
good fortune to be at the novel-reading age in the
fifties.   The future historian of literature may settle
to his own satisfaction what was the permanent value
of the different stars in this constellation, and what
was the relation which George Eliot was to bear to
her competitors.   He will no doubt analyse the spirit
of the age and explain how the novelists, more or less
unconsciously, reflected the dominant ideas which were
agitating the social organism.   I am content to say
that a retrospect, colored perhaps by some personal
illusion, seems to suggest a very comfortable state of
things.   People, we are told, were absurdly optimistic
in those days; they had not learned that the universe
was out of joint, and were too respectable to look into
the dark and nasty sides of human life.   The generation which had been in its ardent youth during the
Reform of 1832 believed in progress and expected the
millennium rather too confidently.   It liked plain
common-sense.   Scott's romanticism and Byron's
sentimentalism represented obsolete phases of feeling,

and suggested only burlesque or ridicule. The novelists were occupied in constructing a most elaborate panorama of the manners and customs of their own times with a minuteness and psychological analysis not known to their predecessors. Their work is, of course, an implicit "criticism of life." Thackeray's special bugbear, snobbism, represents the effete aristocratic prejudices out of which the world was slowly struggling. Dickens applied fiction to assail the abuses which were a legacy from the old order — debtors' prisons, and workhouses, and Yorkshire schools, and the "circumlocution office." The "social question" was being treated by Kingsley and Mrs. Gaskell. But little was said which had any direct bearing upon those religious or philosophical problems in which George Eliot was especially interested. The novelists when they approach such topics speak with sincere respect of religious belief, though they obviously hold also that true Christianity is something very different from the creeds which are nominally accepted by the churches. They regard such matters as generally outside of their sphere, and simply accept the view of the sensible layman with a prejudice against bigotry and priestcraft. Here was one special province for the new writer. George Eliot alone came to fiction from philosophy. She was, as we have sufficiently seen, familiar with the speculations of her day, and had accepted the most advanced rationalist opinions. But, on the other hand, she had a strong religious sentiment which asserted itself the more as she abandoned the dogmatic system. She puts this emphatically in her letters at the time. She had, as she tells M. D'Albert in 1859, abandoned the old spirit

of "antagonism" which had possessed her ten years
before. She now sympathises with "any faith in which
human sorrow and human longing for purity have
expressed themselves." She thinks, too, that Christianity is the highest expression of the religious
sentiment that has yet found its place in the history
of mankind, and has the "profoundest interest in the
inward life of sincere Christians in all ages." She has
ceased, she says a little later, to have any sympathy
with freethinkers as a class, and holds that a "spiritual
blight comes with no faith." It is characteristic that
Buckle, who was startling the world at this time,
inspires her with "personal dislike," as "an irreligious
conceited man." It is therefore intelligible that she
should take a Methodist preacher for her centre of
interest. Methodism, she says, in the opening of
Adam Bede, was a "rudimentary culture" for the
simple peasantry; it "linked their thoughts with the
past," and "suffused their souls with the sense of a
pitying, loving, infinite presence, sweet as summer to
the houseless needy." Methodism, to some of her
readers, may mean "low-pitched gables up dingy
streets, sleek grocers, sponging preachers, and hypo-
critical jargon — elements which are regarded as an
exhaustive analysis of Methodism in many fashionable
quarters." Certainly that would be true of readers of
Dickens. Stiggins and Chadband and their like were
wonderful caricatures, but imply a very summary
"analysis." The difference is significant. George
Eliot had gone much further than Dickens in explicit
rejection of the popular religion, considered as a
system of doctrine; but she found her ideal heroine in
one of its typical representatives.

If, therefore, we accept the author's view, *Adam Bede* is to derive its main interest from Dinah Morris. Her sermon at the opening is to strike the keynote; and we are to share the impression which it makes upon Seth Bede, that "she's too good and holy for any man, let alone me." This view of the book did not strike everybody. The *Saturday Review* contained a "laudatory" but "characteristic criticism." "Dinah," she exclaims, "is not mentioned!" It is "characteristic," no doubt, because in those days the *Saturday Review*, though it had a most brilliant staff of writers, was not distinguished by "enthusiasm," and would be least of all inclined to expend enthusiasm upon a Methodist preacher. There is, we know, a class of beings which has a natural antipathy to holy water. Perhaps it is due to some such weakness that I must confess to a certain sympathy with that unlucky reviewer. Undoubtedly, Dinah Morris is not only an elaborate, but a most skilful and loving portrait of a beautiful soul. Reading the book carefully, one must admit that she performs her part admirably. She shows unerring delicacy and nobility of feeling; and her sermons are expositions of that side of her creed which clearly ought to appeal to one's better nature. I fully admit, therefore, that I ought to accept Seth Bede's estimate, and to fall in love with this undeniable saint, if indeed my reverence ought not to be too strong to admit of love. My failure to do my duty in this respect may possibly be shared by some fellow-sinners. It is true, I think, though perhaps lamentable, that perfect characters in fiction have a tendency to be insipid. One wants some little touch of frailty to convince one that they

are really human.   It was strange, said George Eliot,
that people should fancy that she had "copied"
Dinah. Morris's sermons and prayers, when they were
really "written with hot tears as they surged up in
her own mind."   They have no doubt the earnestness
of genuine feeling.   And yet to me that accounts for
one characteristic without quite justifying it.   Mrs.
Samuel Evans had, one may assume, the defects
incident to her position.   She must have been provincial and ignorant, and the beautiful soul shone
through an imperfect medium.   George Eliot, in
modifying or, as she thought, entirely changing the
"individuality," has deprived her heroine of the
colouring which would make her fully harmonise
with her surroundings.   She is a little too good not
only for Seth but for this world, and I have a difficulty in obeying the summons to fall upon my knees
and worship.

People of happier constitution must accept this as
a confession.   I only wish to explain why I feel myself to be rather at cross purposes with my author,
and to admit that the criticism which I am about
to make may, if not erroneous, be based upon partly
insufficient reasons.   That criticism is briefly that
the development of the story does not quite follow
the lines required by the reader's sympathies.   The
main situation naturally reminds one of Scott's *Heart
of Midlothian*.   Both novels turn upon an accusation of
child-murder, and Jeanie and Effie Deans correspond
roughly to Dinah Morris and Hetty Sorrel.   To "compare" the two, except by admitting that they are both
masterpieces in different styles, would be absurd:
both in their strength and their weakness they are

obviously to be judged by different standards; and I only speak of Scott because his story suggests one significant difference. The interest of the *Heart of Midlothian* culminates in the trial scene where Jeanie Deans has to make the choice between telling the fatal truth or saving her sister by perjury. Scott treats it magnificently in his own way by broad masculine touches. One advantage is naturally offered by the facts from which he started. Jeanie Deans is exposed to a tremendous ordeal, which brings out most effectively her character, and involves a true tragical catastrophe. The scene in the prison, which, as George Eliot tells us, was to be the climax of *Adam Bede*, is curiously wanting in impressiveness of this nature. Poor helpless little Hester Sorrel has been convicted of murder, and expects to be hanged next day. Dinah Morris goes to her in order to persuade her to make a confession. From the point of view of the persons concerned that was no doubt a very desirable result. But it does not in the least matter to the story, as Hetty's guilt has been already conclusively proved. Neither is it a result which requires any great ability for its achievement. Hetty is anything but a criminal who would make a point of "dying game." She is a most pathetic figure, bewildered, deserted, and in immediate prospect of the gallows; and is quite unable to make any opposition to the woman who comes to her with the first message of love from outside her prison. To have failed to extract a confession from her would have shown a singular want of capacity in her spiritual guide. One would have expected that a humdrum gaol chaplain, or a rough revivalist with threats of

hell-fire, could equally have accomplished that end.
Dinah Morris undoubtedly does her duty with admirable tact and tenderness, and shows herself to be —
what we know her to be — a woman with a beautiful
soul. The result, however, is that the real interest
of the scene is with the pathetic criminal, and not
with the admirable female confessor. The story of
Hetty's wanderings in search of her seducer is told
with inimitable force and pathos; and we are not
surprised to learn that it was written continuously
under the influence of strong feeling. Hetty moves
us to the core. Dinah Morris, on the other hand,
instead of forming the real centre of interest, is a most
charming person, who looks in occasionally, and acts
as an edifying and eloquent chorus to comment upon
the behaviour of the people in whom we are really
interested. The last book, therefore, comes upon us,
if we take this view, as superfluous and rather unpleasant. Hetty is despatched to Botany Bay, and we
are suddenly invited to be interested in a new love
affair, when we discover that the saint is not above
marrying, and that Adam Bede, who up to this time
has been passionately in love with Hetty, can be sensible enough to discover the merits of her antithesis.
The tragedy is put aside; all the unpleasant results
are swept away as carefully as possible; and everything
is made to end happily in the good old fashion.

I cannot, therefore, accept *Adam Bede* as centred
upon this religious motive. On that assumption it
ought to have been called *Dinah Morris ;* and the
other characters should have been interesting as
transmitting or resisting the grace which inspires
her. But there all hostile criticism may end. I

can be unfeignedly grateful to the beautiful Methodist
for introducing me to a delightful circle, who were
evoked from George Eliot's early memories. If they
won't stay in the background, I am all the better
pleased. Adam Bede himself is, one is forced to
guess, a closer portrait of her father than she intended. We are told that an old friend of Robert
Evans had the story read to him, and sat up for
hours to listen to descriptions which he recognised,
exclaiming at intervals : " That's Robert, that's Robert to the life ! " No doubt an ordinary reader exaggerates superficial resemblances, and is blind to more
refined differences which seem all-important to the
writer. That the father was one model is undis-
puted; and one remark is suggested by the portrait,
namely, that in spite of her learning and her philosophy, George Eliot is always pre-eminently feminine.
The *Scenes of Clerical Life* suggested, as we have seen,
a dispute as to the sex of the author. Now that we
know, we can, of course, see that others ought to
have showed Dickens's penetration. There is always,
I fancy, a difference which should be perceptible to
acute critics. Men drawn by women, even by the
ablest, are never quite of the masculine gender. They
may, indeed, be admirable portraits, but still portraits
drawn from outside. In each of the clerical stories,
the official heroes are men — Amos Barton, Gilfil, and
Tryan. But in each of them the women — Milly and
Caterina and Janet — are drawn with a more intimate
sympathy; and though a man might have been author
of the heroes, no man, as we may safely say now,
could have described the heroines. Adam Bede is
a most admirable portrait; but we can, I think, see

clearly enough that he always corresponds to the view which an intelligent daughter takes of a respected father. That is, perhaps, the way in which one would like to have one's portrait taken; but one is sensible that the likeness though correct is not quite exhaustive. One characteristic point is the kind of resentment with which the true woman contemplates a man unduly attracted by female beauty. Adam Bede's passion for Hetty produces an exposition of the theory: "How pretty the little puss looks in that odd dress! It would be the easiest folly in the world to fall in love with her," with her "sweet baby-like roundness," "the delicate dark rings of hair," and the "great dark eyes with their long eyelashes." "What a prize the man gets who wins a sweet bride like Hetty!" "The dear, young, round, soft, flexible thing!" A man is conscious of being a great "physiognomist" under such circumstances, and thinks that "Nature has written out his bride's character for him in those exquisite lines of cheek and lip and chin, in those eyelids delicate as petals, in those long lashes curled like the stamen of a flower, in the dark liquid depths of those wonderful eyes!" That was the way in which Adam Bede reasoned, poor man! George Eliot knows better, and suspects "that there is no direct correlation between eyelashes and morals; or else, that the eyelashes express the disposition of the fair one's grandmother, which is on the whole less important to us." In fact, as she truly remarks, "it is generally the feminine eye that first detects the moral deficiencies hidden under the 'dear deceit' of beauty," and Mrs. Poyser is not to be hoodwinked. "She's no better than a peacock, as 'ud strut about on

the wall, and spread its tail when the sun shone if all
the folks i' the parish was dying: there's nothing
seems to give her a turn i' th' inside, not even when
we thought Totty had tumbled into the pit." Mrs.
Poyser, no doubt, is as right as usual, and the remark,
indeed, had been made, like most others, by satirists
of both sexes; but it is specially congenial to the
feminine mind. Miss Brontë, for example, looks on
with similar indignation at the dulness of man when
"Dr. John" in *Villette* is attracted by the frivolous
Ginevra Fanshawe. George Eliot had an eye for the
"kitten-like" beauty of brainless young women, and
her power over the male sex is described as a sort of
natural perversity. "Every man who is not a monster,
a mathematician, or a mad philosopher," she says in
Amos Barton, "is the slave of some woman or other,"
and we must confess the undeniable truth. Strong
men do fall in love with pretty fools. Perhaps we are
not as much ashamed of it as we should be. Hetty
is made so thoroughly charming in her way that we
sympathise with Adam Bede's love for her, and are
quite aware that many precedents might be adduced
for him since the time of Samson. George Eliot thinks
it necessary to apologise, by showing eloquently that
feminine beauty may affect a strong man like music;
and to remonstrate in rather superfluous irony with
the sensible people who despise such weaknesses. No
apology is necessary. Rather we see the point of
Lewes's suggestion. We can perceive that the real
danger was that Adam might be too "passive." His
love for Hetty, we might fancy, is to be passed over
as if it were a painful admission of imperfect sanity.
Luckily the fight with Arthur Donnithorne, when the

flirtation begins to excite suspicion, reassures us. It shows that Adam can really be as great a fool as he ought to be; and afterwards when the whole story comes to light, his agony is as genuine and forcible as we can desire. Adam, in fact, is powerfully drawn from the striking scene, when he sits up at night to finish the coffin left by his drunken father and hears the mysterious stroke of the willow wand which intimates that the father is being drowned, down to the last interview with Hetty after her conviction. The character reacts, as we feel that it ought to react, under the given circumstances. If his later discovery of Dinah's merits does not strike us quite in the same way, we must sorrowfully admit that it is possible. Men do become commonplace and reasonable as they grow older.

Meanwhile, though I have spoken of *Adam Bede* from the point of view suggested by the author's theory, it is neither Dinah Morris nor Adam himself who really made the fortune of the book. *Adam Bede* for most of us means pre-eminently Mrs. Poyser. Her dairy is really the centre of the whole microcosm. We are first introduced to it as the background which makes the " kitten-like " beauty of Hester Sorrel irresistible to young Captain Donnithorne. But Mrs. Poyser is the presiding genius. She represents the very spirit of the place; and her influence is the secret of the harmony of the little world of squire and parson and parish clerk and schoolmaster and blacksmith and carpenter and shepherd and carter. Each of these types is admirably sketched in turn, but the pivot of the whole is the farm in which Mrs. Poyser displays her conversational powers. The little rustic

world is painted in colours heightened by affection.
There is, it may be, a little more of Goldsmith's
beautifying touch than of Crabbe's uncompromising
realism. But it is marvellously life-like, and Mrs.
Poyser's delightful shrewdness seems to guarantee the
fidelity of the portraits. She has no humbug about her,
and one naturally takes it for granted that they must
be as she sees them. It is, indeed, needless to insist
upon her excellence; for Mrs. Poyser became at once
one of the immortals. She was quoted by Charles
Buxton — as George Eliot was pleased to hear — in the
House of Commons before she had been for three
months before the public: "It wants to be hatched
over again, and hatched different." One is glad to
know that Mrs. Poyser's wit was quite original. "I
have no stock of proverbs in my memory," said George
Eliot; "and there is not one thing put into Mrs.
Poyser's mouth that is not fresh from my own mint."
She had written the dialogue with obvious enjoyment,
and appreciated its merits herself. "You're mighty
fond o' Craig," Mrs. Poyser had said "in confidence to
her husband"; "but for my part, I think he's welly
like a cock as thinks the sun's rose o' purpose to hear
him crow." She said it to other people, it seems, for
Mr. Irwine quotes the remark to his mother as one of
the "capital things" he has heard her say. "That is
an Æsop's fable in a sentence," he adds; and he
remarks that Mrs. Poyser is "quite original in her
talk, one of the untaught wits that help to stock a
country with proverbs." It is not often that an author
ventures to praise his own speeches; and that George
Eliot did so shows how much Mrs. Poyser's special wit
was one ingredient of her own intellectual tendency.

In her later novels one sometimes regrets that Mrs. Poyser did not come to the fore to temper the graver moods. Mrs. Poyser may take rank with Sam Weller as one of the irresistible humorists. She has a special gift for attracting us by the most unscrupulous feats of sophistry. Poor Molly breaks a jug, and has been just driven to tears by Mrs. Poyser's eloquence for her unparalleled clumsiness, when Mrs. Poyser repeats the feat, to the amusement of her husband. "It's all very fine to look on and grin," she retorts; "but there's times when the crockery seems alive, an' flies out o' your hand like a bird. . . . What is to be broke *will* be broke, for I never dropped a thing i' my life for want o' holding it, else I should never ha' kept the crockery all these 'ears as I bought at my own wedding." She quenches an outburst of laughter soon after by summoning up a sudden vision of her being laid up in bed, and the children dying, and the murrain coming among the cattle, and everything going to rack and ruin — a prophetic picture which, though logically irrelevant, is most effective rhetorically. Another brilliant specimen of the same figure of speech occurs when she is roused to speak her mind to the squire, who has hinted at giving the farm to a new tenant. "It's a pity," she says, "but what Mr. Thurle should take it, and see if he likes to live in a house wi' all the plagues o' Egypt in 't — wi' the cellar full o' water, and frogs and toads hoppin' up the steps by dozens — and the floors rotten, and the rats and mice gnawing every bit o' cheese, and runnin' over our heads as we lie i' bed till we expect 'em to eat us up alive — as it's a mercy they hanna eat the children long ago." It is superfluous to quote fragments of Mrs. Poyser's familiar

eloquence — spoilt by necessary curtailment — except to
suggest the problem, Why is she so charming? The
answer is, I suppose, in a general way to be found in
the delicious contrast between Mrs. Poyser's intense
shrewdness and strong affections, with the quick
temper and the vivacity with which she snatches at
the most preposterous flights of fancy which will be-
wilder and discomfit her antagonists for the moment.
A logician might amuse himself by analysing her
ingenious arguments. Meanwhile her love for her
husband and the irrepressible Totty — one of the portraits which, without being sentimental, shows George
Eliot's most feminine appreciation of the charms of
childhood — and even her kindness to Hetty, though
she does see through that young woman's weaknesses,
entitles her to the regard felt for her by all readers.
That regard, indeed, is so well established that I am
only using fragments to recall, not to justify the
universal sentiment. I will only note in passing
that a full criticism of *Adam Bede* would have to
touch upon many other subordinate characters. Bar-
tle Massey, for example, the schoolmaster, is, in his
way, an admirable pendant to Mrs. Poyser. Adam
Bede's mother is equally life-like, and the passage in
which she speaks of her wedding was judiciously
noticed by Charles Reade as a masterly touch of
human nature. Seth Bede, I confess, bores me.

If I cannot say, therefore, that *Adam Bede* impresses
me as the author intended it to impress her readers, I
think that by a kind of felicitous accident it came to
be a masterpiece in a rather different sense. The
memory of Mrs. Samuel Evans brought up a vivid
picture of the little world in which she moved; though

her world, as represented by Adam Bede and Mrs.
Poyser themselves, looked upon Methodism as rather
an intruding and questionable force than as the spiritual
leaven which was to redeem it.   George Eliot, meaning to set forth the beauty of Dinah Morris's character,
incidentally comes to draw a more attractive picture
of the sinners whom she ought to have awakened.
Dinah gives up preaching when the Society decides
against the practice, whereas her prototype, it is said,
joined another sect rather than be silenced.   Dinah
settles down by her domestic hearth, and Adam remains a sound Churchman.   He admits in his old age,
we are told, that the excellent vicar, Mr. Irwine,
"didn't go into deep speritial experience," and only
preached short moral sermons.   Apparently Adam
thought none the worse of him.   He quotes Mrs.
Poyser's dictum that Mr. "Irwine was like a good
meal o' victual; you were the better for him without
thinking on it; and Mr. Ryde [his successor] was like
a dose of physic; he gripped you and worreted you,
and after all he left you much the same."   We get the
impression that Mrs. Poyser and Adam took the most
judicious view; and that the rustic congregation, with
its "ruddy faces and bright waistcoats," which reposed
in the great square pews and listened to Mr. Irwine's
moral without attaching any particular meaning to
theological formulæ, did very well without stronger
spiritual stimulants.   "The world," in Sir W. Besant's
formula, "went very well then."   *Adam Bede*, like
Waverley, might have had for a second title *'Tis
Sixty Years Since;* and the verdict seems to be that
the simple society of that period was sound at the
core; wholesome and kindly, if not very exciting.

G

The pathos to be found in commonplace lives was the main topic of the *Scenes of Clerical Life;* and now, looking back with fondness to her early days, and through them to the early days of her parents, George Eliot finds a beauty not in the individuals alone, but in the whole quiet humdrum order of existence of the rustic population. Everybody is treated with a kindly touch. Even the seducer, Arthur Donnithorne, instead of being the wicked baronet who generally appears on such occasions, is a thoroughly amiable, if rather weak, young man, who is not aware of the sufferings of his victim till too late, and then does all he can to obviate unpleasant consequences. "At present," she says, writing a little later, my "mind works with most freedom and the keenest sense of poetry in my remotest past, and there are many strata to be worked through before I can begin to use, *artistically,* any material I may gather in the present." The world of Adam Bede clearly is the world of her first years, harmonised by loving memories and informed, no doubt, with more beauty than it actually possessed. Her philosophy, indeed, reminds her that the range of ideas of her characters was singularly narrow and hopelessly obsolete. She has no sympathy with the romanticism which leads to reactionary fancies. She is perfectly well aware of the darker sides of the past, though she does not insist upon them. She has herself breathed a larger atmosphere. Only her affectionate recognition of the merits of the old world makes one feel how much conservatism really underlay her acceptance, in the purely intellectual sphere, of radical opinions.

The *Scenes of Clerical Life* had made a more decided success with critics than with the public. *Adam Bede* had an equal and triumphant success with both classes. The original agreement with Blackwood had been for £800 for four years' copyright. Seven editions and 16,000 copies were printed during the first year (1859). Blackwood acknowledged the success generously by another check for £800, and gave back the copyright. He offered at the same time £2000 for 4000 copies of her next novel, and proposed to pay at the same rate for subsequent editions. The pecuniary success put her at once and permanently beyond the reach of any pecuniary pressure. Meanwhile she had received hearty greetings on all sides. In April she notes that she has left off recording the "pleasant letters and words" that had come to her: "the success has been so triumphantly beyond anything I had dreamed of, that it would be tiresome to put down particulars." "Shall I ever," she asks herself, "write another book as true as *Adam Bede ?*" The "weight of the future presses on me and makes itself felt even more than the deep satisfaction of the past and present." Old friends had been delighted. One of them, Mme. Bodichon, had discovered the authorship, though she had only inferred it from extracts in the reviews. Her friends the Brays were not so perspicacious, and were "overwhelmed with surprise" when in June she revealed the secret to them. She reopened her acquaintance with M. D'Albert by announcing to him that she had "turned out" to be, like him, "an artist," though in words, not with the pencil. Mr. Herbert Spencer wrote an "enthusiastic" letter, and declared that he felt the better for reading the book. Mrs. Carlyle felt herself in "charity with the whole human race" after the same experience, though her

husband apparently could not be persuaded to try
whether his views of the race could be softened by
the same application.   Letters from Froude and John
Brown of *Rab and his Friends* called forth grateful ac-
knowledgments.   Fellow-novelists were equally warm.
Dickens made her personal acquaintance, and begged
for a novel in *Household Words*.   Charles Reade declared that " Adam Bede was the finest thing since
Shakespeare."   Mrs. Gaskell said how " earnestly, fully,
and *humbly*" she admired both *Adam Bede* and its
precursors.   " I never read anything so complete and
beautiful in fiction in my life before."   Bulwer, with
less expansiveness, pronounced the book to be " worthy
of great admiration," and congratulated Blackwood
upon his discovery.   He thought, it seems, from a
later note, that the defects of the book were the use
of dialect and the marriage of Adam Bede.   " I would
have my teeth drawn," says George Eliot, " rather
than give up either."   One comic incident occurred
amidst this general chorus of praise.   The originals of
some of the descriptions in the novel had been guessed
by people familiar with the neighbourhood ; and in
searching for an author, they had guessed at a Mr.
Liggins, who dwelt in that region.   A Warwickshire
friend, writing to the real author, asked her whether
she had read the books written under the name of
George Eliot, and told her the secret of the Liggins
authorship.   Mr. Liggins, he added, got no profit out
of *Adam Bede*, and gave it freely to Blackwood.   The
incident was not unparalleled.   A young lady, shortly
after this time, made a false claim to one of Trollope's
stories, then appearing anonymously in a magazine.
The claim being taken seriously, she had not the

heart to disavow it; and her father soon afterwards called upon the proprietor to inquire indignantly why his daughter had been allowed to write gratuitously. It does not appear whether Mr. Liggins accepted the authorship or only refrained from a direct disavowal. The claim seems to have caused rather more vexation than was necessary; but the main result was that the secret soon became known. It had been revealed to Blackwood in the previous year (Feb. 1858), soon after the publication of the *Clerical Scenes*.

CHAPTER VI

THE MILL ON THE FLOSS

ADAM BEDE had not been long in the hands of readers when a new novel was begun. At the end of April 1859 George Eliot had finished a short story called "The Lifted Veil"—taken up as "a resource when her head was too stupid for more important work"—and was about to "rewrite" the first two chapters of the novel which ultimately received the name of *The Mill on the Floss*. The first volume was finished before October, the second on 16th January, and the third on 21st March 1860. It appeared at the beginning of April, rivalled *Adam Bede* in its immediate popularity, and sustained or increased her reputation with the most thoughtful readers. In one respect, as already intimated, it is clearly the most interesting of all her books. In the *Scenes of Clerical Life* she had made use of the stories current in the early domestic circle; in *Adam Bede* she had drawn a portrait of that circle itself; and she now took herself for a heroine, and the first two volumes become virtually a spiritual autobiography. The title originally suggested, "Sister Maggie," is really the most appropriate. The external circumstances have, of course, been altered. The scenery is supposed to be in Lincolnshire, and the town of St. Ogg's is said to represent Gainsborough. But her native district still supplies the details. The "round pool," to which she had gone on fishing expeditions with her brother, and the "Red Deeps," which had been a favourite haunt, are transported from Griff to Dorlcote Mill. The attic to which Maggie retires in the mill is the attic to which George Eliot had retired in her father's house. Her brother, we are told, had already detected her in her first story. She was now revealed, not only to him, but to her old neighbours, by the closeness of her descriptions. The important point, however, is her identity with the heroine. The elder Tullivers do not represent her parents; and the brother Tom, it is to be hoped, was at most vaguely suggested by the real Isaac Evans. But Maggie Tulliver, spite of certain modifications — the remarkable personal beauty, for example, which has for good reasons to be bestowed upon her — evidently represents as clearly as possible what George Eliot would have been had she been transplanted in her infancy to some slightly different family in the same district. Although many of the best novels in the language are autobiographical, there is hardly one which gives so vivid and direct a representation of the writer's most intimate characteristics. It is proper, I believe, to speak of such writing as "subjective" — an epithet which sometimes suggests an erroneous inference. Every genuine description is subjective in the sense that it must give the writer's own impressions, and is not a mere adoption of language which has recorded the impressions of others. But it need not be "subjective" in the sense of giving the individual peculiarities alone. Self-knowledge implies also knowledge of our common human nature. The novelist speaks

for us because he speaks for himself. The actual
" confession," of course, depends for its interest upon
the interest of the character revealed; and if that
character be one of great moral and intellectual power,
and an impressive incarnation of an interesting type
of the human species, the direct utterance of its emotions has a peculiar fascination. "To my feeling,"
said George Eliot, "there is more thought and a pro-
founder veracity in *The Mill* than in *Adam;* but *Adam*
is more complete and better balanced. My love of
the childhood scenes made me linger over them, so
that I could not develop as fully as I wished the concluding 'book,' in which the tragedy occurs, and
which I had looked forward to with much attention
and premeditation from the beginning." Bulwer had
made this criticism, and had also found fault with the
scene in which Maggie accepts Tom's dictation too
passively. She admitted that he was right in both
cases, and both remarks were, as we shall see, significant. *The Mill on the Floss*, indeed, considered simply
as a story, obviously suffers from the disproportionate
development of the earlier part; but I do not think
that any reader could wish for a change which would
sacrifice the revelation of character to the requirements
of the plot. Taken by itself, the first part of *The Mill*
represents to my mind the culmination of George
Eliot's power. Maggie is one example of the feminine type which occurs with important modifications
in most of the other stories. But George Eliot throws
herself so frankly into Maggie's position, gives her
"double" such reality by the wayward foibles associated
with her nobler impulses, and dwells so lovingly upon
all her joys and sorrows, that the character glows with

a more tender and poetic charm than any of her other heroines. I suppose that Dinah Morris would be placed higher in the scale of morality; but if the test of a heroine's merits be the reader's disposition to fall in love with her (and that, I confess, is my own), I hold that Maggie is worth a wilderness of Dinahs.

One result of this sympathy with her heroine is conspicuous. No book, I imagine, ever set forth so clearly and touchingly the glamour with which the childish imagination invests the trivial and common-place. There is enough poetry in all of us in our earlier years to enable us to appreciate the truth, though rare genius is required to recall so vividly the old associations and to bring out so tenderly their pathetic side. We all have enough poetry left beneath our layers of commonplace to share Maggie's emotions in the attic, with its high-pitched roof, its worm-eaten floors and shelves, and dark rafters festooned with cobwebs, where she keeps her "Fetish": the trunk of an old doll, into whose head she drives nails in emulation of Jael's feat as pictured in the Family Bible. We can understand, too, the "dim delicious awe" produced by the "resolute din, the unresting motion of the great stones" in the mill, where the meal pours down till the very spider-nets look like a fairy bulwark. Maggie speculated especially upon the "fat floury spiders," and their probable relations to spiders of the outside world. Toads and earwigs become actors in other little romances. She confides to her little cousin that Mrs. Earwig is running so fast to fetch a doctor for a small earwig that has fallen into the hot copper. Brother Tom shows his

matter-of-fact character by smashing the earwig "as
a superfluous yet easy means of proving the entire
unreality" of such a story. The imaginative faculty
transfigures toads and earwigs and invests with mystery the round pool, framed with willows and tall
reeds, where she delights in the "whispers and dreamy
silences," and listens to the "light dipping sounds of
the rising fish and the gentle rustling as if the willows
and the reeds and the water lend their happy whisper-
ing also." Her life is to change, but the old joy can
never be quite lost. "Our delight in the sunshine on
the deep-bladed grass to-day would be no more than
the faint perception of wearied souls if it were not for
the sunshine and the grass in the far-off years which
still live in us and transform our perception into love."

Meanwhile, however, imagination is a faculty which
has its disadvantages when it is placed in uncongenial
surroundings. Its possessor or victim has to suffer
terrible raps over the knuckles from the Tom Tullivers.
"Those bitter sorrows of childhood!" she exclaims,
"when sorrow is all new and strange, when hope has
not yet got wings to fly beyond the days and weeks,
and the space from summer to summer seems measure-
less!" George Eliot insists upon this text, and the
absurdity of telling a child that its real troubles are
to come. "We have sobbed piteously, standing with
tiny bare legs above our little socks, when we have
lost sight of a mother or nurse," but we can no longer
revive the poignancy of the moment. "Surely if we
could recall that early bitterness and the dim guesses,
the strangely perspectiveless conception of life that
gave the bitterness its intensity, we should not pooh
pooh the griefs of our children." I would not ven-

ture to pronounce upon the general soundness of the doctrine; in that matter we all generalise from our private experience, and are very liable to illusions; but the truth for a child of Maggie's peculiarities is undeniable and most pathetic.   When she is not only snubbed by Tom, but roused to jealousy by his kindness to her cousin Lucy, "there were passions at war in her to have made a tragedy, if tragedies were made by passion only; but the essential τι μέγεθος who was present in the passion was wanting in the action; the utmost Maggie could do, with a thrust of her small brown arm, was to push poor little pink-and-white Lucy into the cow-trodden mud."   The remark indicates the curious power of the book.   The chief actors are children, their surroundings are of the dullest and narrowest conceivable, and yet we are spectators of a drama with really tragic interest.   "Not Leonore," we are told, "in that preternatural midnight excursion with her phantom lover, was more terrified than poor Maggie in her entirely natural ride on a short-paced donkey with a gypsy behind her, who considered that he was earning half a crown."   The bray of another donkey under the setting sun becomes portentous, and the low cottages which she passes suggest a probable habitation of witches.

The *Mill on the Floss*, so far, is a singularly powerful presentation, by help of her personal memories, of the theme of Andersen's "ugly duckling"; the seed of genius cast upon barren ground and yet managing to find sufficient nurture from the most unpromising materials.   It is the more effective because the tragic side is not too prominent.   There is none of the brutal tyranny which crushes some children in pathetic fiction. Maggie, on the whole, in spite of all her scrapes, has a good many happy hours, and is child enough to accept the unintentional stupidities of her family circle as part of the inevitable. She is not conscious of being a misunderstood genius; she only suffers because she has vague aspirations and longings, but does not feel herself to be enslaved or bound to overt revolt. The circle, forming the prose element against which her poetic impulses are to struggle, is drawn with a force and humour which, but for the author's distinct disavowal, would convince us that it was a study from the life. Indeed, though we have to admit that there was no actual counterpart of Mrs. Glegg or the Pullets, we must suppose that some of their characteristic traits were taken from real people, though more or less modified and put into different combinations. Certainly we seem to be reading a direct transcript from early recollections when we pay a visit to the Pullets with Mrs. Tulliver and her children, when Mrs. Pullet devoutly exhibits her new bonnet, and is moved by the solemnity of the occasion to thoughts of human mortality. "Ah," she said at last, "I may never wear it twice, sister, who knows?" "Don't talk o' that, sister," answered Mrs. Tulliver; "I hope you'll have your health this summer." "Ah, but there may come a death in the family, as there did soon after I had my green satin bonnet. Cousin Abbott may go, and we can't think o' wearing crape less nor half a year for him." "That *would* be unlucky," said Mrs. Tulliver, entering thoroughly into the possibility of an inopportune decease. The gloom becomes overpowering; and Mrs. Pullet, "beginning to cry," closes the scene worthily by saying, "Sister, if

you should never see that bonnet again till I'm dead
and gone, you'll remember I showed it you this day."
And so they descend to the amiable Mr. Pullet, who
solaces his mind when at a loss for conversation with
lozenges and peppermint-drops, and is the proud
possessor of a musical-box.   His profound respect
for his wife is shown by his memory of the right
time for taking her doctor's stuff.   "There's the pills
as before every other night, and the new drops at
eleven and four, and the 'fervescing mixture' when
agreeable," rehearsed Mr. Pullet, with a punctuation
determined by a lozenge on his tongue.   "Doctor
Turnbull," he adds, "has n't got such another patient
as you in this parish, now old Mrs. Sutton's gone."
"Pullet," says his wife, touched by this delicate compliment, "keeps all my physic bottles — did you know,
Bessy ?   He won't have one sold.   He says it's nothing
but right folks should see 'em when I'm gone.   They
fill two o' the long storeroom shelves already — but,"
she added, beginning to cry a little, "it's well if they
ever fill three.   I may go before I've made up the
dozen o' these last sizes."   The conversation runs on
with such admirable naturalness, that we can but take
it as the echo of such talks as were once the staple of
conversation at Chilvers-Coton.   We may look out
upon old farms as we are hurried past them in the
railway and wonder whether they still shelter Tullivers
and Dodsons, and possibly ask the more inscrutable
question, whether the talk of some ladies nearer
home may not in its essence resemble the remarks
of Mrs. Pullet.

The precious books were meant as revelations of
the romance to be found under the most commonplace

exteriors. It becomes a problem whether this bit of commonplace is not too sordid. It is "irradiated by no sublime principles, no romantic visions, no active self-renouncing faith, moved by none of those wild, uncontrollable passions which create the dark shadows of misery and crime — without that primitive rough simplicity of events, that hard submissive ill-paid toil, that childlike spelling out of what nature has written which gives its poetry to peasant life." George Eliot admits that she shares the sense of oppressive narrowness, but wishes to show how it acted upon the young souls immersed in it. And, after all, she holds that it had its good results. Its religion was simply blind acceptance of tradition, and its morality adherence to established customs. The religion meant going to church on proper occasions; being baptized, because otherwise one could not be buried; and taking care that there should be the "proper pall-bearers and well-cured hams at one's funeral." Mr. Tulliver took much the same view of the services as Tennyson's immortal farmer from the same region. He considered, however, that "church was one thing and common-sense another, and he wanted nobody to tell him what common-sense was." He shows a touch worthy of the "Northern Farmer" when he orders his son to record in the Family Bible a declaration that he will not forgive his enemy, and hopes that evil may befall him. There is a strain of the old Viking blood in him after all, and it is more or less shown in the morality. The Dodsons were "a very proud race"; no one should be able to tax them with a breach of traditional duty. So, even when Mrs. Glegg, the most nagging and contradictory of them all, quarrels with her sister, she

feels bound to leave their fair share of her property
to her sister's children. Their pride was wholesome, as it identified honour with "perfect integrity,
thoroughness of work, and faithfulness to admitted
rules." Mr. Glegg, like his neighbours, was "near";
he had made money very slowly, by steady parsimony,
and saving had become an end in itself. He would
have thought it a "mad kind of lavishness" to give
away a five-pound note to save a poor widow's
furniture, but he was really sorry for her; and was
as anxious to save other people's money as his own.
The Tullivers had warmer hearts and more impulsive
characters than their neighbours, and discharge their
family duties from genuine affection as well as from
a sense of traditional affection. Mr. Tulliver's kindness to his ruined sister atones for his recklessness
and his perverse passion for " lawing "; and his love for
his "little wench " gives her main consolation under
the troubles of her childhood. Her sympathy for him
under his troubles and illness is a natural stage in the
development of her finer qualities.

So far, if it be true that George Eliot's fondness for
the old memories had betrayed her into some disproportionate length, no one can deny the extraordinary skill and force with which the situation is
prepared. We may miss at times the more idyllic
elements represented by Mrs. Poyser's circle, though
the charming pedlar Bob Jakin brings some of the old
wit and quaint humour into the less exhilarating surroundings. At any rate, the mine is very effectually
laid, and we now have to watch the explosion. Maggie,
with her pathetic attempts to snatch at any floating
bits of learning that may enable her intellectual wings

to expand, has gone through her creator's experience in a rather more trying form. She has had to feed upon Defoe's *History of the Devil*, and made attempts to draw honey from the Latin Grammar, Euclid, and Aldrich; and now that a happy chance has introduced her to à Kempis, we can see that she is fitted to receive consolation, under the dry and barren outward life, in some form of religious mysticism. When the sensitive and artistic Philip Wakem, made eager for consolation by his deformity and his own domestic difficulties, meets the beautiful young woman, we are also not surprised that her longings for sympathy should turn to a human object. On both sides there is ample opportunity for awaking love and pity. It is natural, again, that the position should bring her into collision with her brother. He has no turn for poetry and art and mysticism, but his plunge into difficulties has called out the sturdy qualities of the Tulliver race, and we sympathise with his energy in retrieving the family fortunes. The quarrel arises inevitably when he finds that his sister is in love with a youth, not only deficient in the manly qualities, but son and heir to the enemy against whom he has inscribed a vow of vengeance. That he should take a decided course of action under the circumstances is only to be expected. Nor, perhaps, is it surprising that he behaves like a brute. There is plenty of " heredity " to account for that. But here is a first difficulty. George Eliot admitted, as I have said, that the scene between brother and sister was not quite satisfactory. The young woman, with her high-wrought enthusiasm, submits too " passively," not to say, tamely, to his imperious inter- ference. She confesses that she has done wrong, and promises not to see her lover again in private. Tom's behaviour, I fancy, makes him simply offensive to most people, though it seems to be obvious that we are intended to retain a certain regard for him. The failure seems to me to be easily explicable. I heard once from a most intelligent lady of an elder generation that the agitation for women's rights was absurd, because as a matter of fact all women like, and always will like, to be slaves. Younger ladies, it is true, have assured me that this is a complete mistake, and that women have as strong an objection as men to be objects of tyranny. I should be afraid to express any opinion upon a question in which women must be the best judges. Yet I am half inclined to guess that, along with other conservative tendencies, George Eliot had inherited some sympathy with this older view. Of course, she would be the last person to approve the tyranny of brothers or husbands, and is only trying to do justice to the moral code accepted in St. Ogg's circles, of which it was a part that the family should be under masculine supremacy. The true difficulty is again, as I take it, that she was too thoroughly feminine to be quite at home in the psychology of the male animal. Her women are — so far as a man can judge — unerringly drawn. We are convinced at every point of the insight and fidelity of the analysis; but when she draws a man, she has not the same certainty of touch. She is, I have suggested, a little too contemptuous when the Samson yields to the Delilah; and when he asserts his privileges, his strength is apt to be too like brutality. Many rustic Tom Tullivers would, no doubt, ride roughshod over sisterly sensibilities; but if we are to retain sympathy for

H

their better nature, they should show more twinges
of conscience.   Tom's profound conviction that whatever he does is therefore right, is no doubt characteristic; but he might at least feel that he is doing a
painful duty, and not be represented as utterly in-
sensible to the claims of the old childish affections.

The comparative weakness, however, of masculine
portraits has a more unpleasant result. She admits that
the tragedy which follows is "not adequately prepared."
She will " always regret" the want of fulness in the
treatment of the third volume, due, as she says, to the
epische Breite into which she was beguiled by love of
her subject in its predecessors.   But she defends the
position itself, which many readers have condemned.
" Maggie's position towards Stephen Guest — upon
which the tragedy turns — is," she says, " too vital a
part of my whole conception and purpose for me to be
converted to the condemnation of it.   If I am wrong
there — if I did not really know what my heroine
would feel and do under the circumstances in which I
deliberately placed her — I ought not to have written
this book at all, but quite a different work, if any.   If
the ethics of art do not admit the truthful presentation of a character essentially noble, but liable to great
error — error that is anguish to its own nobleness —
then it seems to me the ethics of art are too narrow,
and must be widened to correspond with a widening
psychology."   Without discussing the " ethics of art,"
we may, I should think, fully agree that the critical
canon thus abjured is erroneous.   I am not aware,
however, that any professor of æsthetics has laid
down the rule that it is wrong to represent a noble
character led into fatal error, and consequent remorse,

by its weaknesses. I should have supposed that
nothing could be a more legitimate topic. George
Eliot is unintentionally changing the issue upon which
a defence is really required. We have sympathised
keenly with Maggie. We understand the "strange
thrill of awe" which passes through her when passages
from the *Imitation of Christ* affect her like a strain of
solemn music; when she infers that "the miseries of
her young life had come from fixing her heart on her
own pleasure"; and saw the possibility of looking at
her own life as "an insignificant part of a divinely
guided whole." She forms "plans of self-humiliation
and entire devotedness, and fancies that renunciation
will give her" the satisfaction for which she had so long
been "craving in vain." "She had not perceived —
how could she until she had lived longer? — the inmost
truth of the old monk's outpourings that renunciation remains sorrow, though sorrow willingly borne.
Maggie was still panting for happiness, and was in
ecstasy because she had found the key to it." That is
beautifully said, and is followed by an admirable account of her effort to attain the true spirit. When,
again, Philip Wakem urges her not to stifle human
affections, and persist in a "narrow asceticism," and
assures her that "poetry and art and knowledge are
sacred and pure," we can quite see the force of the argument, and understand why it should be the prologue to
a love-scene a little later. After an appeal from Philip,
Maggie at last "smiled with glistening tears, and
then stooped her tall head to kiss the pale face that
was full of pleading, timid love like a woman's. She
had a moment of real happiness then — a moment of
belief that, if there were sacrifice in this love, it was

all the richer and more satisfying." The "renunciation" and the desire for happiness may be reconciled.

With Tom Tulliver in the background, we have
now abundant material for tragedy. But, at the
opening of the third volume, we are abruptly introduced to a new character. Maggie has become a young
lady, visiting her cousin. The "fine young man,"
snapping a pair of scissors in the face of the "King
Charles" spaniel on Miss Lucy Deane's feet, "is no
other than Mr. Stephen Guest, whose diamond ring,
attar of roses, and air of nonchalant leisure at twelve
o'clock in the day are the graceful and odoriferous
result of the largest oil-mill and the most extensive
wharf in St. Ogg's." In other words, Mr. Guest is a
typical provincial coxcomb, with a certain taste for
music, fitted no doubt to excite the admiration of young
ladies at St. Ogg's. No attempt is made to suggest
that he is anything but a self-satisfied commonplace
young gentleman, who has condescended to accept the
hand of Miss Deane. There is no difficulty in understanding him and his manners. When he dances
with Maggie at a ball soon afterwards, and takes her
into a conservatory, she looks very lovely as she
stretches her arm to a rose. "Who has not felt the
beauty of a woman's arm? — the unspeakable suggestions of tenderness that lie in the dimpled elbow, and
all the varied gently lessening curves, down to the
delicate wrist with its tiniest almost imperceptible
nicks in the firm softness? A woman's arm touched
the soul of a great sculptor two thousand years ago, so
that he wrought an image of it for the Parthenon which
moves us still as it clasps lovingly the time-worn marble
of a headless trunk. Maggie's was such an arm as that,

and it had the warm tints of life. A mad impulse
seized on Stephen; he darted towards the arm and
showered kisses on it, clasping the wrist." It is
curious that a little later (1864) George Eliot describes a "divine picture" by Sir F. Burton, in which
a mailed knight is kissing the arm of a woman "by an
uncontrollable movement." The subject, she says, is
from a "Norse Legend." It "might have been made
the most vulgar thing in the world — the artist has
raised it to the highest pitch of refined emotion. The
kiss is on the fur-lined *sleeve* that covers the arm, and
the face of the knight is the face of a man to whom the
kiss is a sacrament." Mr. Stephen Guest's performance
does not strike one in the sacramental light. Maggie
is properly angry and astonished at the time, but
she soon becomes more amenable; and though she has
scruples, and goes through a "fierce battle of emotions,"
she presently finds herself drifting to sea with him in a
boat, and is only arrested by her conscience at the last
moment when she is some way towards Gretna Green.
Renunciation gets the better of the longing for happiness. " We can only choose," she says, "whether we will
indulge ourselves in the present moment, or whether
we will renounce that for the sake of obeying the
divine voice within us, for the sake of being true to
all the motives that sanctify our lives." To let this
belief go would be to lose the only light in the dark-
ness of life. She returns; but the knot is insoluble,
and has to be finally cut by the waves of the Floss.
George Eliot herself, admitting the need for more
development, maintained, as we have seen, that the conclusion was right, and it has been defended upon the
same ground. It is right, because the " psychology "

is right. Given the character and the circumstances,
that is, this was the inevitable outcome. It is, no
doubt, painful and disagreeable that a young woman
of so many noble qualities should be guilty of such a
step; but noble young women do make slips — that, I
fear, is undeniable — and Maggie behaves as might be
expected from her previous history. That is where I
presume to doubt. Nobody, indeed, can deny that
the passion of love is apt to generate illusions. Most
men would probably be able to give examples from
their own experience of the truth that young women
who fall in love with somebody else have a singular
inability for forming a correct judgment of the truly
valuable qualities of masculine character. The fact
has often been noticed, and is frequently turned to
account by novelists. I will not deny that even
Maggie's love for Stephen is conceivable. A young
woman brought up in Dorlcote Mill was no doubt
liable to be imposed upon by a false appearance of
gentlemanlike character. But, one thing seems to be
obvious. The whole theme of the book is surely the
contrast between the "beautiful soul" and the commonplace surroundings. It is the awakening of the
spiritual and imaginative nature and the need of
finding some room for the play of the higher faculties,
whether in the direction of religious mysticism or of
human affection. That such a character, with little
experience of life and with narrow education, should
fall into error is natural, if not inevitable. But then
the error should surely correspond to some impulse
which we can feel to be noble. Maggie may be
wrong in attributing high qualities to her hero; but
we should feel that, in her eyes, he has high qualities,

and that the passion, if misdirected, is itself congenial
to her better impulses.   Miss Brontë's heroines fall in
love with men whom the reader may dislike; but it is
because they take the men to be embodiments of great
masculine qualities — energy, honour, and real generosity — under rather crusty outsides. Therefore, though
we may doubt the perspicacity of the hero-worship, we
do not feel that the sentiment is in itself degrading.
But there is this difficulty with poor Maggie.   Her
admiration for Mr. Guest would be natural enough in
the average miller's daughter suddenly brought into
a rather superior social scale and introduced to a well-
dressed young man scented with "attar of roses."
But as Maggie, by her very definition, as one may say,
is a highly exceptional young woman, she should surely
have something exceptional in her love.   We can
understand her sympathy with Philip Wakem, who is
a man of heart, and whose physical infirmity is an
appeal for pity; we could have understood it if she
had fallen in love with the excellent vicar of St. Ogg's,
who would have been able to talk about à Kempis and
religious sentimentalism; and we might even have
forgiven her if, after being a little overpowered by the
dandified Stephen, she had shown some power of perceiving what a very poor animal he was.   The affair
jars upon us, because it is not a development of her
previous aspirations, but suddenly throws a fresh and
unpleasant light upon her character.   No one will
say that the catastrophe is impossible; he, at least,
who would pronounce dogmatically upon such matters
must be a bolder man than I am; but neither, I think,
can any one say that it was inevitable, or could have
been expected, given the circumstances and the

characters. The truth is, I think, different. George
Eliot did not herself understand what a mere hair-
dresser's block she was describing in Mr. Stephen
Guest. He is another instance of her incapacity for
portraying the opposite sex. No man could have
introduced such a character without perceiving what
an impression must be made upon his readers. We
cannot help regretting Maggie's fate; she is touching
and attractive to the last; but I, at least, cannot help
wishing that the third volume could have been sup-
pressed. I am inclined to sympathise with the readers
of *Clarissa Harlowe* when they entreated Richardson
to save Lovelace's soul. Do, I mentally exclaim, save
this charming Maggie from damning herself by this
irrelevant and discordant degradation.

CHAPTER VII

SILAS MARNER

GEORGE ELIOT had not yet exhausted the materials of her early recollections. In the autumn of 1860 she wrote a short story called *Brother Jacob*, of which, as of its predecessor, *The Lifted Veil*, nothing need be said. But in the November of that year she began *Silas Marner*, which was finished in February 1861, and appeared by itself in March. Blackwood, she says, does not surprise her by calling it "rather sombre." She would not have expected it to interest any one except herself (" since Wordsworth is dead ") had not Lewes been "strongly arrested" by it. The reference to Wordsworth is explained by her statement that it is meant to "set in a strong light the remedial influences of pure natural human relations." She felt as if it would have been more suitable to metre than to prose, except that there would have been less room for the humorous passages. It was suggested, it seems, by a childish recollection of a "linen-weaver with a bag on his back." The recollection, it must be admitted, can have counted for very little in the development of a story which is often considered to be her most perfect artistic performance. A curious literary coincidence — it can have been nothing more — is mentioned by Mathilde Blind. The Polish novelist,

Kraszewski, wrote a novel called *Jermola, the Potter*, said to be his masterpiece, and to have been translated into French, Dutch, and German. Jermola is an old servant who has retired to a deserted house in a remote village. He becomes almost apathetic in his solitude, till one day he finds a deserted infant under an oak. He devotes himself to the care of the child, and is helped in the unfamiliar process of nursing by a kind old woman. His energies revive, he takes up the trade of a potter to make a living for his new charge, succeeds in the business, and is brought into friendly relations with his neighbours. Finally, the child's parents turn up and reclaim their son. Jermola has to submit, but afterwards runs off with the boy into the forests. There the child dies of hardship, and Jermola ends his days as a melancholy hermit. The treatment, says Miss Blind, is entirely different from that of *Silas Marner*, but the leading motive is identical, and some of the details have, as will be seen, a curiously close resemblance. As there is clearly no question of copying, we must infer that both writers have worked out the logical consequences of similar situations; Kraszewski's version is more " sombre," though either his catastrophe or that of George Eliot is equally conceivable. The supposed event—the moral recovery of a nature reduced by injustice and isolation to the borders of sanity—strikes one perhaps as more pretty than probable. At least, if one had to dispose of a deserted child, the experiment of dropping it by the cottage of a solitary in the hope that he would bring it up to its advantage and to his own regeneration would hardly be tried by a judicious philanthropist. That, perhaps, is the reason which made George Eliot think

it more appropriate for poetry. In an idyll in verse
one is less disposed to insist upon prosaic probabilities,
or apply the rules of life suggested by the experience
of the Charity Organisation Society. In *Silas Marner*
George Eliot is a little tempted to fall into the error
of the amiable novelists who are given to playing
the part of Providence to their characters. It is true
that the story begins by a painful case of apparent
injustice. Silas Marner's life has been embittered by
the casting of lots, which, on the principles of his sect,
proves him to be guilty of the crime really committed
by his accuser. But in the conclusion Providence
seems to be making up for this little slip. The child
is given to the weaver to recompense him for his
sufferings, and, conversely, the real father is punished
for neglecting his duty by the childlessness of his
second marriage and the refusal of his daughter to
accept him in place of her adopted parent. The
excellent Dolly Winthrop sees a difficulty. She holds
that the parson could probably explain the mistake
about the casting of lots, though even he would have
to tell it in " big words." But she is convinced that
" Them above has got a deal tenderer heart than what
I have." " There is plenty of trouble in the world,
and things as we can never make out the rights on.
And all as we 've got to do is to trusten, Master
Marner — to do the right thing as far as we know, and
to trusten." If Marner had acted on that principle, he
would n't have " run away from his fellow-creatures
and been so lone." I will not quarrel with Mrs.
Winthrop's solution of the ancient problem, nor with
the moral which she deduces; and if the conclusion
of the story seems to imply that compensation for

injustice may be expected in this life rather more confidently than experience proves, another moral is also
suggested. Mr. Godfrey Cass is driven to prevarica-
tion and lying in order to conceal from his father that
he has made a disreputable marriage, and to prevent
his scamp of a brother from ousting him by revealing
the result. His meanness answers admirably. The
brother tumbles into a gravel-pit and is drowned, and
the wife takes an overdose of laudanum at the right
moment. He is freed from all fear of exposure,
marries the right young woman, and has, on the
whole, a successful life. This may console people who
think that the justice of Providence is called into play
too clearly. But in truth the whole story is conceived
in a way which makes a pleasant conclusion natural
and harmonious. It is saved from excess of sentimentalism by those admirable passages of humour,
which, as we have seen, prevented the story from being
put into verse. *Silas Marner*, as it turned out, was to
be the last work in which George Eliot was to draw
an idealised portrait of her earliest circle. It is full of
admirable sketches from the squire to the poor weaver;
and the famous scene at the "Rainbow" is perhaps the
best specimen of her humour. The condescending
parish clerk and the judicious landlord and the con-
tradictious farrier, with their discussions of village
traditions, their attempts at humour, and the curious
mental processes which take the place of reasoning,
are delicious and inimitable. One secret is that we can
sympathise with their humble attempts at intellectual
intercourse. The brutality which too often underlies
a good deal of more refined satire comes out in the
"unflinching frankness," which at the "Rainbow" is

taken for the "most piquant form of joke." The pre-
sumption of the assistant clerk, who hopes that he
may have his own opinion of his vocal performances, is
tempered by the remark that "there'd be two opinions
about a cracked bell if the bell could hear itself," and
finally crushed by the critic who tells him that his
voice is "well enough when he keeps it up in his nose."
It's your inside "as isn't right made for music; it's
no better nor a hollow stalk." Much of the wit that
passes current in more elegant circles differs from this,
less in substance, than in the skill with which the
sarcasm is ostensibly veiled. When Charles Lamb proposed to examine the bumps on the skull of an illiterate
person, he was just as rude, though his rudeness is
allowed to pass for harmless fun. The crude attempts
of the natural man are redeemed from brutality by
the absence of real ill-nature. So the argument as to
reality of ghostly phenomena is a tacit parody upon a
good deal of the controversy roused by "Psychical research." Some people, as the landlord urges, couldn't
see ghosts, "not if they stood as plain as a pikestaff
before 'em." My wife, as he points out, "can't smell,
not if she'd the strongest of cheese under her nose. I
never see a ghost myself; but then I says to myself,
very like I haven't got the smell for 'em. I mean,
putting a ghost for a smell, or else contrairiways.
And so, I'm for holding with both sides." The farrier
retorts by asking, "What's the smell got to do with
it? Did ever a ghost give a man a black eye? That's
what I should like to know. If ghos'es want me to
believe in 'em, let 'em leave off skulking in the dark,
and i' lone places — let 'em come in company and
candles." "As if ghos'es 'ud want to be believed in

by anybody so ignirant!" replies the parish clerk.
We have read something very like this, only expressed
in the "big words" which Mrs. Winthrop left to the
parson.   One touch of blundering makes the whole
world kin; and in these good people, with their
primitive views of logic and repartee and their quaint
theology, we may, if we please, see a satire upon their
betters. Rather, if we accept George Eliot's view, we
have a kindly sympathy for the old order upon which
she looked back so fondly.   A modern "realist"
would, I suppose, complain that she had omitted, or
touched too slightly for his taste, a great many repulsive and brutal elements in the rustic world.   The
portraits, indeed, are so vivid as to convince us of
their fidelity; but she has selected the less ugly, and
taken the point of view from which we see mainly
what was wholesome and kindly in the little village
community.   *Silas Marner* is a masterpiece in that
way, and scarcely equalled in English literature, unless
by Mr. Hardy's rustics in *Far from the Madding Crowd*
and other early works.

The novels hitherto noticed suggest an interesting
comparison. M. Brunetière in his study of the *Roman
Naturaliste* infers from them that George Eliot is the
type and the founder of English "naturalism."   English novelists are hardly to be classified in separate
schools so distinctly as their French rivals; and I
fancy that M. Brunetière slightly exaggerates the importance and extent of the new departure.   Scott, for
example, though called a "romantic," is as much a
"naturalist" in his descriptions of Dandie Dinmont or
Edie Ochiltree as George Eliot in her Adam Bede or
Tulliver.   But M. Brunetière shows admirably the

peculiar merits of the "English naturalism" which she represented. Her profound psychology, he says, her metaphysical solidity and her moral breadth, are displayed in that sympathetic treatment of the commonplace and ugly upon which I have had to insist. Sympathy of the heart and the intelligence is "the soul" of this "naturalisme." It preserved her, as M. Brunetière points out, not only from the coarse brutalities of M. Zola, but from the scorn for the *bourgeois* in which he finds the weak side of Flaubert's *Madame Bovary.* This is the great set-off against the superior skill in unity of composition and thorough finish of style which must be allowed to be a French characteristic. I will not try to expand a criticism which shows a true appreciation of George Eliot's most admirable quality. I will only add that in a comparison of George Eliot with French writers much would have to be said of George Sand, whom she had read with such enthusiasm, and in whose stories of French country life we may find the nearest parallel to *Silas Marner.* But though the affinity between the two great feminine novelists is sufficient to explain George Eliot's appreciation of her rival's sentiment and passion, it does not seem to have suggested any appropriation of artistic methods. One palpable difference is that while George Sand poured forth novels with amazing spontaneity and felicity, each of George Eliot's novels was the product of a kind of spiritual agony. Some consequences, good or bad, of George Eliot's method will become conspicuous.

CHAPTER VIII

MIDDLE LIFE

THE publication of *Silas Marner* marks an important change in the direction of George Eliot's work. The memories of early days are no longer to be the dominant factor in her imaginative world; and henceforth one charm disappears; however completely, to the taste of some readers, it may be replaced by others. She has begun, as we have seen, to consider theories about the relations of ethics and æsthetics and psychology; and hereafter the influence of her theory upon her writing will be more obvious. This brings one in sight of certain general canons of criticism, upon which I do not desire to touch any further than is necessary for an appreciation of George Eliot herself. Yet the moral and philosophical implications of her novels are so prominent that it is impossible to omit altogether one or two questions as to their propriety. Many critics seem to lose their temper at any suggestion that a poem or a novel can have any legitimate didactic purpose. Everybody must sympathise with their annoyance. It is undeniably vexatious to take up a novel and find that it is a pamphlet in disguise, and that the envelope of fiction merely coats the insipid pill of a moral platitude. We have all suffered from such well-meant impositions in our childhood; "we," I mean, who

were born in the good old days when children read
the *Parent's Assistant* and *Hymns for Infant Minds.*
Somehow many of the old stories with a moral were
very delightful. I am still grateful to the author
of *Sandford and Merton,* though I fear that I did not
assimilate the ethical teaching of the excellent Mr.
Barlow. The objection, however, expresses a most
undeniable and indeed painfully obvious proposition.
There is, beyond all dispute, a fundamental distinction
between the literature of the imagination and the
literature of science. "We need not say," observes
the historian of King Valoroso, "that blank verse is not
argument." A novelist's facts can prove nothing, for
the simple reason that they are fictions; and his narrative, when it is reasoning in disguise, becomes intolerable. But still we must ask, What is a poor novelist to
do who happens to have been impressed by some of the
great masters of thought, such as Plato or Spinoza,
whose philosophies are embodied poetry? Is he to
forget all the thoughts that have occurred to him in
his philosophical capacity, and to write as though he
had no more speculations about the world or human
nature than the most frivolous of his readers?
If his "philosophy" has really modified his own
microcosm, can he drop it when he describes the
world? And why should he be called upon to
drop it? Must he not, at any rate, have some tinge
of psychology? When Fielding wrote *Tom Jones,*
the first great English novel upon modern lines, he
announced that he took "human nature" for his
subject; and all his successors have aimed, according
to their capacity, at providing us with studies of the
same subject from different points of view. We might

I

describe this by saying that fiction must be applied
psychology.   The phrase, no doubt, would startle
innocent readers who fear the intrusion of some
hideous scientific doctrine.   Yet it is a way of stating
a harmless commonplace.   Shakespeare was, no doubt,
a very different writer from Professor Bain.   He did
not write a treatise upon the *Emotions and the Will;*
but when he described Hamlet, he imagined a character
which forcibly illustrates the relation between those
faculties.   The merit of the character depends upon
the insight, and therefore upon the correctness of the
psychology, though Shakespeare had not read Bain,
nor even Bacon, and had never thought of the possibility of any such science, or of taking a scientific view
at all.   To George Eliot, of course, various psychological theories, Mr. Herbert Spencer's and others,
were familiar.   They were too familiar, we may fancy,
when in defending Maggie Tulliver she appeals, as I
have said, to the desirability of conforming to enlightened expositions of modern psychology.   That
may suggest a possible danger — the danger of constructing her characters out of abstract formulæ
instead of reversing the process.   But certainly it was
not any abstract theory that taught her that a girl of
Maggie's character would be likely to comfort herself
with the mysticism of à Kempis, or to fall in love with
Stephen Guest.   She simply knew the fact from her
own experience or her observation of others.   But not
the less, we may say without offence that her insight
is justified by psychology, and that Maggie, like
Hamlet, is profoundly interesting — not because her
character has been constructed from psychological
formulæ, but because when presented it offers prob-

lems to the psychologist as fascinating as any direct autobiography. The truthfulness goes far beyond any explanation from our crude guesses at the appropriate scientific formulæ. The imaginative intuition presents the concrete reality which no theorist can analyse into its constituent elements, and we can recognise, though we cannot logically prove, its fidelity and subtlety. Nor need we really be frightened by the " philosophy." There is a rather quaint entry in her diary about this time : " Walked with George over Primrose Hill. We talked of Plato and Aristotle." We may dread a possible intrusion of disquisitions upon the theories of those sages into the uncongenial sphere of fiction as well as into familiar talk. But, so far as we have yet gone, I cannot perceive any ground for offence of that kind. George Eliot was a " philosopher " in the sense that she had reflected long and seriously with all her very remarkable intellectual power upon some of the greatest problems which can occupy the mind. She had, in particular, thought of the part which is played by the religious beliefs and their real meaning and value. She had accepted, more or less, a particular system, though hitherto at least she made no special reference to it, and certainly did not change her novels into propagandist manifestoes. What, in fact, she had acquired was a cordial respect and sympathy for creeds embodied even in crude and superstitious dogmas; and she had, therefore, described many types, which in less thoughtful minds suggested only absurdities and provoked caricatures, with the intention of laying stress upon the nobler aspirations of such humble people as Silas Marner and Dolly Winthrop. If by "philosophy" we understand some metaphysical system constructed by logical subtlety, it has certainly no direct relation to poetry; but if it corresponds to that state of mind in which the varying beliefs and instincts, even of the vulgar, have been considered with a desire to understand and appreciate their value, then it is likely, I fancy, to give harmony and sympathetic warmth to pictures of human life. George Eliot's merit in these novels is just proportioned to our sense that we are looking through the eyes of a tender, tolerant, and sympathetic observer of the aspirations of muddled and limited intellects.

This suggests one other stumblingblock. George Eliot speaks, we have seen, of the "ethics of art," and to some people this appears to imply a contradiction in terms. Æsthetic and ethical excellence, it seems, have nothing to do with each other. George Eliot repudiated that doctrine indignantly, and I confess that I could never quite understand its meaning. The "ethical" value of artistic work, she held, is simply its power of arousing sympathy for noble qualities. The "artist," if we must talk about that personage, must, of course, give true portraits of human nature and of the general relations of man to the universe. But the artist must also have a sense of beauty; and, among other things, of the beauty of character. He must recognise the charm of a loving nature, of a spirit of self-sacrifice, or of the chivalrous and manly virtues. He shares, indeed, with the scientific observer the obligation of seeing things as they are; and must not only admit the prevalence of evil, but see even what "soul of goodness" is to be found in things evil. He must be as absolutely impartial as the physiologist describing the physical organisation.

But the impartiality does not imply insensibility. The fairest statement of the facts ought, if our morality be sound, to bring out the beauty of the moral character most fully. In fact, the charm of all the great novelists, from Cervantes downwards, consists essentially in the power with which they have drawn attractive heroes, and won love both for them and their creators. If anybody holds that morality is a matter of fancy, and that the ideal of the sensualist is as good as that of the saint, he may logically conclude that the morality of the novelist is really a matter of indifference. I hold myself that there is some real difference between virtue and vice, and that the novelist will show consciousness of the fact in proportion to the power of his mind and the range of his sympathies. Whether, as a matter of fact, novels do exert much ethical influence is another question; and the answer depends a good deal upon the character of the readers. But I cannot doubt that one secret of George Eliot's power lay in a sympathy with many types in which was essentially implied a power of responding spontaneously to noble and tender sentiment.

George Eliot's theory of the relation of novels to morality appears to me to be so far essentially sound. It must be admitted, however, that theories are dangerous things. They become shackles or suggest erroneous applications of power. They are dangerous to the spontaneity which marks a true imaginative inspiration. The writer who wishes to enforce some moral maxim is apt not only to pervert facts, but to force his humour. He cudgels his brain into framing illustrations which he takes for proofs. When this error is avoided, even the most direct didactic intention may cease to be mischievous. Richardson's novels, for example, were gigantic tracts, written deliberately and intentionally to enforce certain moral doctrines. That did not prevent *Clarissa Harlowe* from being one of the great novels of the world, nor was the *Nouvelle Héloïse* of his disciple, Rousseau, less important on account of its didactic purpose. It does not matter so much why a writer should be profoundly interested in his work, nor to what use he may intend to apply it, as that, somehow or other, his interest should be aroused, and the world which he creates be a really living world for his imagination. This suggests the difficulty about George Eliot's later writings. The spontaneity of the early novels is beyond all doubt. She is really absorbed and fascinated by the memories tinged by the old affections. We feel them to be characteristic of a thoughtful mind, and so far to imply the mode of treatment which we call philosophical. Her theories, though they may have guided the execution, have not suggested the themes. A much more conscious intention was unfortunately to mark her later books, and the difficulties resulted of which I shall have to speak.

The Leweses had lived at 8 Park Street, Richmond, from 1855 till the end of 1858. They then moved to Holly Lodge, where she formed an intimate friendship with the Congreves. Mr. Congreve was a leading member of the Positivist Society, which had much of her sympathy in the following years. In 1860, after the publication of the *Mill on the Floss*, they moved again to 16 Blandford Square. The union with Lewes had involved a breach with many of her early friends, and in some cases the separation was obviously painful. She declares that it was never a trial to her to have been cut off from what is called the "world," and thinks that she "never loved her fellow-creatures the less for it." Still she has a "peculiar regard" for those who stood by her at the time. "The list of those who did so," she adds, "is a short one, so that I can often and easily recall it." She explains a few days afterwards that she has made it a rule never to pay visits. "Without a carriage, and with my easily perturbed health, London distances would make any other rule quite irreconcilable for me with any efficient use of my days, and I am obliged to give up the *few* visits which would be really attractive and fruitful in order to avoid the *many* visits which would be the reverse." Other reasons for the same course are obvious; but those mentioned were, no doubt, genuine and sufficient. The rest of her life was passed with very little indulgence in society. Lewes's children formed part of the household, though they were mainly educated abroad. They were on thoroughly affectionate terms with her; and, for the most part, she led a quiet domestic life, finding her chief recreation in music. She read, she says, slowly; but she read much, eschewing most modern literature of the lighter kind, and absorbing very thoroughly what she did read. The *Life*, afterwards published by Mr. Cross, was made upon the plan, no doubt the right one, of telling her story from her own letters. There were, however, few incidents to be told; and Lewes undertook most of her correspondence. One result is that comparatively little is told in her letters of her later mental history. A great part of the correspondence

consists of accounts of holiday tours, which cannot be
said to have any remarkable interest. In 1860, after
finishing the *Mill on the Floss,* she made a three
months' tour in Italy. Visits to Italy have been a
turning-point in the lives of many great English
writers; and this tour had, as we shall see, a very
important effect upon George Eliot. The diary and
letters, however, in which it is described leave a
disappointing blank. The Leweses saw Rome, Naples,
Florence, Venice, Milan, and other famous places;
went most conscientiously through all the regular
sights; and, of course, made plenty of judicious and
intelligent remarks. In Florence, for example, they
admire " Brunelleschi's mighty dome " and " Giotto's
incomparable campanile." They visit the palaces and
the churches, and we have a list of the art treasures
which specially attract them in the Pitti Palace and
the Uffizi Gallery. In the Pitti Palace " there is a
remarkably fine sea piece by Salvator Rosa; a striking
portrait of Aretino, and a portrait of Vesalius by
Titian; one of Inghirami by Raphael; a delicious rosy
baby — future cardinal — lying on a silken bed; a placid
contemplative young woman, with her finger between
the leaves of a book, by Leonardo da Vinci " — and
so forth. No doubt it is all true; only one has read
something very like it before; and with the help of
Baedeker and Murray one might make out such a list
without being a great author. Of course, it would be
absurd to infer that George Eliot did not receive many
impressions which she did not confide to her diary. I
must, however, confess that there is, to my mind,
something characteristic in the docility with which she
accepts the part of the intelligent sightseer. There

are plenty of appreciative remarks; but none of those brilliant flashes with which Ruskin could light up the well-worn topics of descriptive enthusiasm, and couch our dull eyes to new aspects of familiar beauties. We feel that the man of genius gives his personal impressions, which are, therefore, more or less governed by accident or prejudice, but which, nevertheless, extort a partial assent, and at the lowest make us more vividly conscious of one element in our emotions. George Eliot, so far as this diary goes, seems to be simply recording the verdicts already pronounced by the most enlightened and respectable authorities.

CHAPTER IX

THE inference which I have just suggested may seem
to be contradicted by facts. While at Florence George
Eliot conceived "a great project," of which she wrote
to Blackwood during her homeward journey. She is
anxious to keep it secret, and it will require a great
deal of "study and labour," but she is "athirst
to begin." The project, as she shortly afterwards
explains, is for a historical novel, the scene to be
Florence, and the period that of Savonarola's career.
She postponed the work, however, till she had finished
Silas Marner, and then made another visit to Florence
in the spring of 1861. She spent thirty-four days
there in May and June, devoting the morning hours
to "looking at streets, books, and pictures, in hunting
up old books at shops and stalls, or in reading at the
Magliabecchian Library." She feels "very brave,"
and enjoys the thought of work. "It may turn out,"
she adds, "that I can't work freely and full enough
in the medium I have chosen, and in that case I must
give it up; for I will never write anything to which
my whole heart, mind, and conscience don't consent;
so that I may feel it was something — however small
— which wanted to be done in this world, and that
I am just the organ for that small bit of work."

Nobody, it may safely be said, could have undertaken a great task in a more conscientious spirit. She was, as usual, tormented by "hopelessness and melancholy." In August I "got," she says, "into a state of so much wretchedness in attempting to concentrate my thoughts on the construction of my novel, that I became desperate, and suddenly burst my bonds, saying, I will not think of writing." A week later, however, she conceives her plot "with new distinctness." Gradually she gets to work, and "crams" — if the word may pass — with amazing diligence. A list of the books which she read during the last half of 1861 gives some illustration of the course of study. Among them are Villari's and Burlamacchi's lives of Savonarola, Machiavelli, Petrarch, and other Italian authors, Sismondi's history of the Italian republics, besides various excursions into Gibbon, Hallam, Heeren, and Muratori, and occasional digressions into other literary regions. She began *Romola* "again" on January 1, 1862, and a note of three weeks later is suggestive. She has been "detained from writing by the necessity of gathering particulars, first, about Lorenzo de' Medici's death; secondly, about the possible retardation of Easter; third, about Corpus Christi Day; fourthly, about Savonarola's preaching in the Quaresima of 1492." She also finished *La Mandragola* — a second reading for the sake of Florentine expressions — and began *La Calendra.* The question will intrude, What would have become of *Ivanhoe* if Scott had bothered himself about the possible retardation of Easter? The answer, indeed, is obvious, that *Ivanhoe* would not have been written. One of the results to George Eliot of this excessive conscientiousness is what might be anticipated. She has looked

into some of the notebooks in which she recorded her
former fits of depression; "but," she says, "it is
impossible for me to believe that I have ever been
in so unpromising and despairing a state as I now
feel." She has, however, made a start, and is as usual
encouraged by Lewes's applause.

Soon after this George Smith, the eminent pub-
lisher, offered £10,000 for the copyright of the new
novel, of which some report had got abroad. He
wished it to appear in the *Cornhill Magazine*, which
was still in its brilliant youth. Thackeray was just
retiring from the editorship, but he and many others
of the most eminent writers of the day were still
contributors. George Eliot had only written about
sixty pages of her story, and was still in the depths of
depression. She doubted whether it would ever be
finished or ever good for anything. Offers of £10,000
are cheering even to the most high-minded authors.
Greater sums have been made by successful novelists
in recent years, but at that time the proposal was one,
as Lewes said, of "unheard-of magnificence." She
declined it at first on the ground of her unwillingness
to begin the publication at the early date first fixed by
Smith (May). Afterwards, however, she accepted
£7000 for its appearance in the *Cornhill*, where it
accordingly came out in fourteen parts, from July
1862 to August 1863. She had finished the last
number on the 9th June 1863. Lewes advised her to
accept this periodical mode of publication, because he
thought that the book would have the advantage of
being studied slowly and deliberately, instead of being
read at a gallop. It is understood that the experiment
was not a success in the magazine from the com-

mercial point of view. To make up in some degree
for this disappointment, she made a present to the
Cornhill of *Brother Jacob* — the short and not very
satisfactory story previously written. *Romola* was not
well adapted for being broken up into fragments, and
some people, it appears, evaded Lewes's ingenious trap.
They waited till the work came out as a whole, or
preferred not reading it at all to reading it " slowly."
Perhaps it was too good for an audience of average
readers. She received a great deal of pretty encouragement "from immense big-wigs — some of them
saying that *Romola* is the finest book they ever read."
Some " big-wigs " were less enthusiastic, but the more
orthodox opinion was that *Romola* was a literary
masterpiece, though full recognition of its merits was
a proof of superior taste. The success, to whatever it
amounted, had been won at a heavy cost. She felt at
times as though she were working under a heavy
leaden weight. The writing " ploughed into her "
more than any of her other books. She began it, she
said, as a young woman, and finished it as an old
woman.

It would be absurd to speak without profound
respect of a book which represents the application of
an exceptionally powerful intellect carrying out a
great scheme with so serious and sustained a purpose.
The critic may well be unwilling to place himself in
the seat of judgment, or to suppose that he can divine
with any confidence what will be the opinion of
posterity, if that vague and multitudinous body
troubles itself to arrive at any definite opinion on the
matter. On the other hand, it is not very difficult to
say what one thinks oneself, and one may hope to

suggest a remark or two which may be worth at least the trouble of refuting. *Romola* is to me one of the most provoking of books. I am alternately seduced into admiration and repelled by what seems to me a most lamentable misapplication of first-rate powers. I will speak frankly on both topics, without pretending to reach a precise valuation of merits.

The "historical novel" is a literary hybrid which is apt to offend opposite sides. Either the historian condemns it for its inaccuracy, or the novel-reader complains of its dulness. It is hard to avoid that Scylla and Charybdis. In my youth, I remember that classical students used to pore over two lively works, *Gallus* and *Charicles,* which represented the efforts of a German professor to empty a dictionary of classical antiquities into the framework of a novel. They were no doubt accurate, but I don't know whether anybody ever read them through. Scott's historical romances, on the other hand, fascinated the world, but are generally marked by a gallant indifference to any quantity of anachronisms. A historical critic, I suppose, would tear *Ivanhoe* to pieces, and forbid any student to read a book which would confuse his ideas in direct proportion to the literary attractiveness. Of course, we may request the historical critic to mind his own business. I have often thought that the beginning of *Ivanhoe,* the scene in the forest where Gurth and Wamba are chatting at the foot of the old barrow, and encounter the Templar and the Prior on their way to Cedric's house, is the best opening of a story ever written. It is inimitably graphic and picturesque, and introduces us at once to a set of actors most dramatically contrasted. Moreover, the

interest does not flag till certain unfortunate con-
cessions to the old-fashioned rules of story-telling
spoil the concluding scenes. Still it is true that the
indifference to accuracy, or even possibility, forces one
to admit that it requires a rather juvenile readiness to
accept the obvious unrealities. It suggests the thought
that the charm might be even heightened if, for example, Robin Hood and Friar Tuck had a little stronger
resemblance to real or at least possible outlaws. The
problem had been attacked by two or three of George
Eliot's contemporaries. Bulwer in *Rienzi* had, like
George Eliot, found a theme in Italian history, besides
dealing with Harold and with Warwick the *Last of the
Barons*. Though Freeman admired *Harold*, and George
Eliot read *Rienzi* respectfully, I do not suppose that
these rapid dashes into a mixture of fiction, history,
and political philosophy can now interest any one.
Kingsley in *Hypatia* and *Westward Ho!* had shown
abundant vigour as a story-teller, in spite of a large
infusion of the religious and political pamphleteer;
but did not convince readers that he had given the
true spirit of his periods. Charles Reade's remarkable
novel *The Cloister and the Hearth*, which appeared in
1861, was a more serious attempt to make general
history into fiction, and has been greatly admired by
some eminent critics, such as Mr. Swinburne, who
possibly have in mind the comparison with *Romola*.
I only mention these books, however, to justify the
remark that, in a period when the serious study of
history was developing, the attempt to combine the
vigour of Scott with more thorough knowledge of
facts represented a very natural and plausible enterprise.

It may be taken for granted that the first condition
of success is that you should become a contemporary
of the society described. It is no easy task to go
back for some centuries; to immerse yourself so
thoroughly in the extinct modes of thought and
sentiment that you can instinctively feel what the
actors would have felt under the supposed circumstances. You can see into the mind of a British rustic
of sixty years ago, especially if you happen to have
been his daughter; but to get back to the inhabitant
of Florence in the fifteenth century requires a more
difficult transformation. Did George Eliot achieve it
even approximately? To that, as it seems to me,
there can be but one answer. She saw most clearly
that the feat was necessary. She tried to qualify
herself most industriously, but the very nature of her
preparation shows the extreme difficulty, or, as I think,
the impracticability of the task. " She spent," says
an admiring critic, " six weeks " (really seven) " in
Florence in order to familiarise herself with the
manners and conversation of the inhabitants." In
spite of this, it is said, her characters, when she began
to write, not only " refused to speak Italian to her,
but refused to speak at all." By hard reading, however, she reduced " these recalcitrant spirits to order,"
and " succeeded so well, especially in her delineation
of the lower classes, that they have been recognised
by Italians as true to life." The Italians are
an eminently intelligent as well as an eminently
courteous people; and we will hope that these
anonymous critics had not to put any great strain
upon their consciences. Yet one cannot help contrasting this initiation into the Italian characteristics

with the unconscious process which had lasted for twenty years at Chilvers-Coton. Seven weeks is a brief period for acclimatisation in a new social atmosphere. If an intelligent Italian lady had spent seven weeks at the Charing Cross Hotel, walked diligently about Leicester Square and the Strand, read steadily at the British Museum, and rummaged old bookshops in back streets, how much knowledge would she have acquired of the British costermonger? No doubt with the help of a few books on London labour, and study of Sam Weller's cockney slang, she might manage to make him talk and behave himself in such a way that a critic could not put his finger upon any directly assignable blunder. There is, too, a certain likeness between human beings everywhere, which might save the costermonger from being a mere monstrosity. But one would not expect a very vivid realisation of the genuine Englishman; nor can I see any indications that the description of the Italian "lower classes" in *Romola* gets beyond careful observance of costume and commonplace. George Eliot had not, like some novelists, been primarily interested in a period, steeped her mind in its literature simply for the love of it, and then felt a prompting to give form to her impressions. "They," said Scott, speaking of certain imitators, "have to read old books and consult antiquarian collections to get their knowledge. I write because I have long since read such works, and possess, thanks to a strong memory, the information which they have to seek for."[1] George Eliot had, it is to be presumed, a fair knowledge of the general outlines of history. She came to Florence as a highly intelligent

[1] *Journal*, i. 275.

K

sightseer; and it then struck her that "the place would make a picturesque background, and that the Savonarola period offered a number of interesting situations. She proceeded to get up the necessary knowledge; but with the result like that which happens when a manager presents *Julius Cæsar* or *Coriolanus* in the costume "of the period." The costume may be as correct as the manager's archæological knowledge allows, but Julius Cæsar and Coriolanus remain what Shakespeare made them, not ancient Romans at all, but frankly and unmistakably Elizabethans.

Meanwhile the attempt to be historically accurate has a painfully numbing effect on her imagination. She seems to be always trembling at the possibility of an intruding anachronism. She tells an admirable critic, R. H. Hutton, that "there is scarcely a phrase, an incident, an allusion [in *Romola*] that did not gather its value to me from its supposed subservience to my main artistic purpose." She always strives after as full a vision of the medium in which a "character moves as of the character itself. The psychological causes which prompted me to give such details of Florentine life and history as I have given are precisely the same as those which determined me in giving the details of English village life." That, no doubt, is perfectly true; but then she had seen the English details with her own eyes, and she only makes a judicious selection from authorities when describing Florentine details. There was, it appears, an article of dress called a "scarsella," which always gets upon my nerves in *Romola*. The thing will intrude without any (to me) perceptible relation to her "main artistic purpose." The scarlet waistcoats and brand-new white smock-frocks in *Adam*

Bede make a picture at once. We see the rustics on their way to the squire's feast; but this wretched scarsella worries me, and only suggests a hint for Leighton's illustrations. A more important result of this weakness is shown in another case defended by George Eliot herself. She complains that "the general ignorance of old Florentine literature" and other causes have led to misunderstandings of many parts of *Romola* — "the scene of the quack doctor and the monkey, for example, which is a specimen not of humour as I relish it, but of the practical joking which was the amusement of the gravest old Florentines, and without which no conception of them would be historical. The whole piquancy of that scene in question was intended to lie in the antithesis between the puerility which stood for wit and humour in the old republic, and the majesty of its front in graver matters." She appeals to the precedent of the chase of the false herald in *Quentin Durward*, which makes Louis XI. and Charles of Burgundy "laugh even to tears." Now, I am quite unable to speak of the historical accuracy. All one can say is that if the ancient Florentines laughed so heartily at the dreary joke of imposing a monkey upon a quack for a baby, they must have been duller than one would have supposed. The precedent from Scott is curiously inapplicable. The scene in *Quentin Durward* is effective and an essential part of the story, because the "joke" shows both the brutality of the performers and the cunning of Louis XI. The king is skilfully getting rid of a cast-off agent in his intrigues against Charles with the help of Charles himself. To detail a wearisome practical joke in all its native unadulterated badness in

order to make a contrast with other parts of the book
is a hazardous experiment. It is to be deliberately
dull, because history proves that people could be dull
four centuries ago. The truth is that in her English
books George Eliot can make bad joking amusing,
because she makes us smile not at the joke, but at the
jokers. The talkers at the "Rainbow" are inimitable,
because their talk is so pointless. Here the incongruity which is to interest us has to be gradually
inferred from subsequent reflection, and the writer
falls into the common error of boring us by describing bores.

These are trifling illustrations of the more general
difficulty. *Romola* is to give us the spirit of the
Renaissance. It requires no dissertation to show
why the Renaissance should have a surpassing charm
for the imagination. There is, I suppose, no book
which opens the eyes of the respectable modern reader
with more startling effect than the autobiography of
Benvenuto Cellini in the next generation. The combination of artistic inspiration, intellectual audacity,
gross superstition, and supreme indifference to morality, gives the shock of entering a new world where
all established formulæ break down, or are in a chaotic
state of internecine conflict. When we take up a book
in which one is to be a contemporary with the Borgias,
and to have personal interviews with Machiavelli,
we may expect a similar sensation. We are to be
spectators of a state of things in which the element-
ary human passions have been let loose, when violence
and treachery are normal parts of the day's work, where
new intellectual horizons have opened, and yet the
old creeds are still potent, and there is the strangest

mingling of high aspirations and brutal indulgence, when the nobler and baser elements of belief are so strangely blended that the ruffian is still religious, and the enlightened reformer fanatically superstitious. If anybody derives any vivid impressions of such a world from *Romola,* his eyes must be much keener than mine. George Eliot has, it must be noticed, chosen one of the two alternatives which are open to the historical novelist. She deals with a private history and the great public characters, and their political proceedings remain for the most part in the background. Savonarola, indeed, has to act in the story as well as in the history. Hutton considers the portrait of the reformer to be one of George Eliot's great triumphs, and appeals especially to one scene. I am the more glad to be able to point to an appreciative and genial criticism, as I have to confess my inability to accept it. I should have taken the same scene for the clearest illustration of failure. The prophet is in his cell. He is trying to make up his mind to accept the test proposed by his enemies. Representatives of both parties are to walk through fire, counting upon a miraculous intervention; the flames are to burn the heretic and spare the orthodox. Savonarola's enthusiasm prompts him to run the risk; but when he tries to imagine the scene, the flesh shrinks, he begins to suspect that the appeal may be presumptuous, and is well aware at the bottom of his mind that it is a trap devised by his enemies. To show Savonarola tortured by these conflicting impulses would no doubt require the highest dramatic genius. What we really have is not the concrete man at all, but a long and very able psychological analysis of his mental state. A

bit of it gets into inverted commas to pass for a soli-
loquy; but instead of seeing and hearing Savonarola,
we are really listening through several pages to a
highly intelligent lecture upon an interesting specimen.
The style becomes cumbrous and flagging. I venture
to quote a long sentence as a specimen of George Eliot
at her worst. The acceptance of the ordeal is inevitable : "Not that Savonarola had uttered and written
a falsity when he declared his belief in a future supernatural attestation of his work; but his mind was so
constituted that while it was easy for him to believe
in a miracle which, being distant and undefined, was
screened behind the strong reasons he saw for its
occurrence, and yet easier for him to have a belief in
inward miracles such as his own prophetic inspiration
and divinely-wrought intuitions, it was at the same
time insurmountably difficult to him to believe in the
probability of a miracle which, like this of being carried
unhurt through the fire, pressed in all its details on his
imagination and involved a demand not only for belief
but for exceptional action." Savonarola's mind was
surely, in this respect, constituted like most people's;
we all think that we can bear the dentist's forceps till
we get into his armchair; but this almost Germanic
concatenation of clauses not only puts such obvious
truths languidly, but keeps Savonarola himself at a
distance. We are not listening to a Hamlet, but to a
judicious critic analysing the state of mind which
prompts "to be or not to be." The same languor
affects all the historical framework of the story. We
come upon many scenes which seem to demand a
forcible presentation : the entry of the French into
Florence; the "bonfire of Vanities"; and the strange

tragicomedy of the ordeal; but when we want to see
the crowd and bustle and the play of popular fun and
passion, we get careful narrative; and as half of it —
we do not know which half — is obviously only fiction,
we think that we might as well have been reading
Guicciardini or Professor Villari. The story of the
political intrigues is necessary to determine the fate
of the characters; but it is as dull as any of the
ordinary history books. Machiavelli talks, but he
talks like a book, and does not manage one really good
bit of Mephistophelian cynicism. The great men of
Florence seem to be as prosy when they are feasting
as when they are playing practical jokes. One of them
receives credit for " short and pithy " speech to which
the "formal dignity " of his interlocutor is an amusing
contrast. This short and pithy gentleman manages to
take a page to say that he takes the Savonarola party
to be composed of psalm-singing humbugs, not to be
trusted by men of sense.

If my irreverence reveals a real defect in my author
instead of myself, I think that the defect is explicable.
George Eliot, I have suggested, was a woman; a woman,
too, of rather delicate health, exhausted by hard work;
and, moreover, a woman who, in spite of her philosophy,
was eminently respectable, and brought up in a quiet
middle-class atmosphere. " To bring in a lion among
ladies is a most dreadful thing," we know, "and there
is not a more fearful wildfowl than your lion living."
Benvenuto Cellini would certainly have been " a fearful
wildfowl" in St. John's Wood; and though by dint of
conscientious reading George Eliot knew a great deal
about the ruffian geniuses of the Renaissance, she
could not throw herself into any real sympathy with

them. Such a feat required the audacity of a Victor Hugo and, perhaps, the indifference to propriety of a modern realist. The criticism would be summed up by calling the book " academic "; meaning, I take it, that it suggests the professor's chair ; and implies the belief that a careful study of authorities, and scrupulous attention to æsthetic canons, will be a sufficient outfit for a journey into the regions of romance. George Eliot was not blind to such considerations; and George Lewes, in his capacity of critic, could put them very keenly in writing of other people. His enthusiastic admiration for George Eliot perhaps obscured to him what he would have been the first to see elsewhere ; and, anyhow, he encouraged her tendencies to a questionable direction of her genius.

Yet I do not deny that there was much to be said for the judgment of the contemporary critics who held that *Romola* would be one of the permanent masterpieces of English literature. Before I can adjust my own impressions to theirs, I must be allowed to remove from my mind any lingering impression that Romola and Tito lived at Florence in the fifteenth century. They were only masquerading there, and getting the necessary " properties " from the history-shops at which such things are provided for the diligent student. Romola was, I take it, a cousin of Maggie Tulliver, though of loftier character, and provided with a thorough classical culture. The religious crisis through which she had to pass was not due to Savonarola, but to modern controversies. The antagonistic principles which were in conflict in the Renaissance period are still in existence, though they have entered into different combinations, and are

tested by different issues.   There are still Machiavel-
lians, I believe, in politics, and Epicureans in art and
morals, and the tender soul still finds something of the
charm in the Catholic ideal of life which appealed to
Romola through Savonarola.   If, therefore, we venture
to drop the history, or to consider it as a mere conventional background, we can still be interested in the
real subject of the book, the ordeal through which
Romola has to pass, and the tragedy of a high feminine
nature exposed to such doubts and conflicting impulses
as may still present themselves in different shapes.   I
could wish, indeed, that there were a good deal less history, or that it had been handled with more audacity.
But for all that, Romola and her immediate surroundings
make a very impressive group, which may affect us like
some masterpiece in which a painter has made use of
conventional and unreal accessories.   The central idea,
or, if we choose to say so, the "moral" of the book, is
clearly indicated.   The pressing problem for Romola,
we are told, when she comes under the influence of
Savonarola, is not to settle questions of controversy,
but "to keep alive that flame of unselfish emotion by
which a life of sadness might well be a life of active
love."   She is so moved by the "grand energies" of
the prophet's nature that she can listen patiently even
to his prophecies.   She is profoundly impressed in the
scene in which he comes nearest to being a living person ; and tells her that to run away from her husband
is really to be self-willed and moved by selfish purposes.
She is to "make her marriage-sorrows an offering"
and to live for Florence, where she has been placed
by God, who addresses her through her teacher.   The
light abandonment of ties because they have ceased

to be pleasant is "the uprooting of social and personal virtue." Her marriage has ceased to be for her the "mystic union which is its own guarantee of indissolubleness"; and there is no compensation "for the woman who feels that the chief relation of her life has been no more than a mistake." She has lost her crown. The deepest secret of human blessedness has half whispered itself "to her and then for ever passed away." She accepts the position till presently even Savonarola ceases to command her confidence. She finds that he can hoodwink his conscience for the benefit of his sect. "No one who has ever known what it is to lose faith in a fellow-man whom he has profoundly loved and reverenced will lightly say that the shock can leave the faith in an Invisible Goodness unshaken." Romola despairs of finding any consistent duty. "What force was there to create for her that supremely hallowed motive which men call duty, but which can have no inward constraining existence through some form of constraining love?" The solution, so far as there is one, comes in a form which one cannot altogether admire. Poor Romola, in her despair, gets into a miscellaneous boat lying ashore; and the boat drifts away in a manner rarely practised by boats in real life, and spontaneously lands her in a place where everybody is dying of the plague, and she can therefore make herself useful to her fellow-creatures. She clearly ought to have been drowned, like Maggie, and we feel that Providence is made to interfere rather awkwardly. Perhaps, too, Romola's sentiments show rather too clearly that she has been prematurely impressed by the Positivist "religion of humanity." But a fine nature torn by conflicting duties and ideals, and

IX.]   *ROMOLA*   139

endeavouring to find some worthy conciliation, presents an admirable theme, and often enables George
Eliot to show her highest powers of delineation. Readers in general cannot feel quite so warmly to Romola
as to the childish Maggie; she is a little too hard and
statuesque, and drops her husband rather too coolly
and decisively as soon as she finds out that he is
capable of disregarding her sentiments. Still she is
one of the few figures who occupy a permanent and
peculiar niche in the great gallery of fiction; and if
she is a trifle chilly and over-dignified, one must admit
that she is not the less lifelike. She is, moreover, the
only one — to my feeling — of George Eliot's women
whose marriage has not something annoying. She
marries a thorough scoundrel, it is true, but the misconception to which she falls a victim is one which we
feel to be thoroughly natural under the circumstances.
Her husband, Tito, is frequently mentioned as one of
George Eliot's greatest triumphs. The cause of her
success is, as I take it, that Tito is thoroughly and
to his fingers' ends a woman. I do not intend to
condemn the conception, for undoubtedly there are
men whose characters are essentially feminine. Tito
is of the material of which the Delilahs are made, the
treacherous, caressing, sensuous creatures who involve
strong men in their meshes as Tito fascinates the rather
masculine Romola. In several of her novels George Eliot
contrasts the higher feminine nature with this lower
type. Dinah Morris is relieved against the "kitten-
like" Hetty; Maggie against Lucy Deane; and Dorothea against Celia Brooke; and in *Romola* itself we
have Tessa, who, indeed, is so much of a kitten that
she approaches very nearly to be an idiot. Tito is the

kitten, or rather the panther-cub, grown to full size,
and showing all the grace and malignity of his kind.
He has the feminine nervousness, and " trembles like a
maid at sight of spear and shield." When he catches
sight of an enemy with a dagger, his face at once
commends itself to a painter for the exhibition of the
passion of fear. He is not cruel out of mere badness,
but from effeminacy ; he dislikes the sight of suffering, and would rather not inflict it where he must be
a witness of it; but he can suppress the sympathy
instead of the suffering, and does not mind how much
his victims suffer so long as they are out of his sight.
He has " a native repugnance to sights of death and
pain," and would rather get rid of an enemy by exiling
him than by putting him to death. But when the
sentence is passed, he is comforted by reflecting
upon the security which will come to him when the
enemy's head is well off his shoulders. He is so
thoroughly feminine that we have to be reminded
that he could on occasion show " a masculine effec-
tiveness of intellect and purpose." When he is fairly
driven into a corner, that is, he can show his claws
and act, for once, like a man. But his general position among his more violent associates is like that
of a beautiful and treacherous woman who makes
delicate caressing and ingenious equivocation do the
work of the rougher and more downright masculine
methods. He is most admirably adapted to impose
upon his high-minded wife, who has the reluctance
to admit suspicion which marks noble and simple
characters, but is also apt, unfortunately, to imply
a deficiency of common sense. The tragedy which
follows for Romola is inevitable, and is developed

with George Eliot's full power. If we can put
aside the historical paraphernalia, forget the dates
and the historical Savonarola and Machiavelli, there
remains a singularly powerful representation of an
interesting spiritual history; of the ordeal through
which a lofty nature has to pass when brought into
collision with characters of baser composition; thrown
into despair by the successive collapses of each of the
supports to which it clings; and finding some solution
in spite of its bewilderment amidst conflicting gospels,
in each of which truth and falsehood are strangely
mixed. There is hardly any novel, except the *Mill on
the Floss,* in which the stages in the inner life of a
thoughtful and tender nature are set forth with so
much tenderness and sympathy. If Romola is far less
attractive than Maggie, her story is more consistently
developed to the end. She may remind us of another
heroine who once set everybody weeping — although
the histories of the two are in most respects diametri-
cally contrasted. Clarissa Harlowe had very different
troubles to undergo; she was too well instructed in
the doctrines of the Church of England to be bothered
by any religious doubts; and the respectable society
in which she was brought up had no affinity to the
Renaissance. The similarity is chiefly confined to
the fact that both stories have a moral and a unity
of interest, dependent upon a model young woman as
the central figure, but there is one other resemblance:
Clarissa's troubles, like Romola's, raise the question
whether the moral conventions of the society in which
she lives have a sanctity which should forbid the
individual woman ever to defy them on behalf of
her own happiness. It is curious that upon that

point George Eliot seems on the whole to agree with
Richardson. Romola is perplexed by the thought that
the " law is sacred," but that " rebellion may be sacred
too." There are moments in life when the soul must
dare to act on its own " warrant," though the punish-
ment may be incurred if the warrant has been false.
Clarissa incurs all her troubles by running away from
home, and Romola by her revolt against her husband ;
and though Romola finally escapes with her life, she
has to suffer a heavy penalty. It is only, however,
upon the general point that I mean to insist. Hardly
any heroine since Clarissa has been so effective a centre
of interest as Romola ; and if I regret that she was
moved out of her own century and surrounded by a
mass of irrelevant matter of antiquarian or sub-histori-
cal interest, I will not presume to quarrel with people
who do not admit the incongruity.

CHAPTER X

FELIX HOLT

GEORGE ELIOT had first become known as a writer (by
" Amos Barton ") in January 1857. When the concluding part of *Romola* appeared within six years, she had
reached the first rank among her contemporaries. She
had published within that time five novels of the highest
excellence, and it is at least doubtful whether she was
ever again to reach an equally high mark. The effort
had been very great, and for the next two years she
seems to have allowed her mind to lie fallow. Then
she took up a new book, of which I shall have to speak
presently, although nothing was published until 1866.
In November 1863 the Leweses settled at the Priory,
21 North Bank, Regent's Park. This house came to
be especially associated with her memory. She
did not go out into society; but many people were
attracted by the fame of the great authoress, and
found admission to her house. Gradually she came
to hold a Sunday afternoon reception, frequented by
worshippers of genius and by a large circle of friends,
of whom only the more intimate had the privilege of
seeing her upon other days. It is needless to say that
at meetings of that kind — in England at least, for we
are told that in France things are better — there is
often a painful sense of awkwardness. The shyness

143

generated by the desire to prove that your homage is
genuine, and that you are so brilliant a person that
it is also worth having, gives one of those painful
sensations which is not least among the minor miseries
of life. It may, I think, be said that the evil was
reduced to a minimum on those occasions at the
Priory. George Lewes, in the first place, was un-
quenchable. He was always full of anecdote and
vivacious repartee; and while more serious interviews
were taking place at the centre of the circle, there
would be a little knot on the periphery which was a
focus of laughter and good-humoured fun. It was a
rather awful moment for the neophyte when he was
presented to the quiet and dignified lady seated in
her armchair, to stammer out the appropriate remarks
which sometimes failed to present themselves before
he had to make room for a new comer; and if the
company was numerous, any general conversation was
impossible. George Eliot's gentle voice was not calculated, if she had desired such a result, to hold the
attention of a roomful of receptive admirers. But if
rainy weather had limited the audience, and the tenta-
tive sparks of conversation had been fanned into life,
she could be as charming as any admirer could desire.
Her personal appearance was intellectually attractive,
and had a peculiar pathetic charm. She looked fragile,
overweighted perhaps by thought, and with traces
of the depression of which she so often complains in
her letters. Her abundant hair, auburn-brown, in
later years streaked with grey, was covered by a kind
of lace mantilla. She could not be called beautiful.
She was said to be like Savonarola, of whose face she
remarks : " It was strong-featured, and owed all its

refinement to habits of mind and rigid discipline of the body." His gaze impressed Romola because it was one " in which simple human fellowship expressed itself as a strongly-felt bond." That at least might be applied to George Eliot. Her features were strongly marked, with a rather large mouth and jaw; her eyes a grey-blue, with very variable expression; her hands were finely formed; her voice low and very musical — " a contralto," it is said in singing; and the whole appearance expressive of a singular combination of power with intense sensibility. The best likeness is that by her friend Sir Frederick Burton, now in the National Portrait Gallery. If her talk might be at times a little too solemn for the frivolous, she could brighten into genuine playfulness, and, on occasion, into flashes of hearty scorn directed against the unlucky cynic. If the incense offered was not always of the finest quality, there was no want either of dignity or gentleness in the recipient. And nobody could watch Lewes on such occasions without being struck by the cordial and generous devotion of a man not too much given to an excess of veneration. Her belief in him was equally visible in her manner and every allusion to his work.

It is perhaps not altogether healthy for any human being to live in an atmosphere from which every unpleasant draught of chilling or bracing influence is so carefully excluded. Lewes performed the part of the censor who carefully prevents an autocrat from seeing that his flatterers are not the mouthpiece of the whole human race. " It is my rule," said George Eliot, " very strictly observed, not to read the criticisms on my writings. For years I have found this

abstinence necessary to preserve me from that discouragement as an artist which ill-judged praise no
less than ill-judged blame tends to produce in me.
For far worse than any verdict as to the proportion
of good and evil in our work is the painful impression
that we exist for a public which has no discernment
of good and evil." She spoke with a contempt for
the average quality of contemporary criticism which —
as the critics whom we now call contemporary belong
to a different generation — I might perhaps venture to
approve.   But it might be an interesting question for
an essayist whether this rule of mental hygiene be
really sound.   Since the days when Pope writhed
under the insults of Grub Street, sensitive authors
have called upon gods and men to pity and avenge
them.   Their moanings seem to be rather unmanly.
Which is the proper comment upon the supposed
slaughter of Keats : Shelley's denunciation of the
" deaf and murderous viper," who could crown

> " Life's early cup with such a draught of woe " :

or Byron's comment —

> " 'Tis strange the mind, that very fiery particle,
>   Should let itself be snuffed out by an article " ?

I fancy that in these days, when authors subscribe
to agencies for newspaper cuttings, the general verdict
would be in favour of Byron.   It would be regarded,
that is, as a contemptible weakness to be thrown off
one's balance by a "scathing" review.   Yet, it may
be asked, if one really despises, is one bound to read ?
It is unpleasant to be insulted even by a fool, and
why expose oneself to a pain which can have no

good results? Such abnormally sensitive poets as Tennyson and Rossetti suffered cruelly from harsh criticism, and it is not clear that they gained anything from reading it. Would they not have done better if they could have adopted George Eliot's method? After all, what does a real genius ever learn from a critic? There is, it seems to me, only one good piece of advice which a critic can give to an author, namely, that the author should dare to be himself. When he proceeds to tell the author what the self really is, he is generally mistaken, and is speaking upon a topic upon which he is presumably worse informed than the person to whom he speaks. George Eliot worked upon her own theories, right or wrong; and considering the constant diffidence and depression from which she suffered, it is likely enough that a study of the critics would only have discouraged her without at all directing her into a better path. Against this, it may perhaps be urged that George Eliot's talent scarcely included the rare gift of a just appreciation of her own limitations. It is often, and, no doubt, justly said, that one of Jane Austen's especial merits is that she never let herself be distracted from the sphere in which she showed unsurpassed felicity. When she was requested to write a romance to illustrate the history of the "august house of Coburg," she judiciously declined, and indeed refrained from less palpably absurd divagations. Now George Eliot, as I shall presently have to remark, showed what most people have thought to be — if not so great a misconception, still — a conspicuously erroneous estimate of her own special peculiarities. Perhaps, though she closed her ears to "deaf and murderous vipers," she

listened with too much complacency to adoring and
" genial " critics who collected her " wise, witty, and
tender sayings," and took her for a great poet
and philosopher as well as for a first-rate novelist.
I will not affect to sum up the argument. It is only
worth remarking that most novelists who have given
effective portraits of human passion have lived in the
world which they described, and that some characteristics of George Eliot's later work must be connected
with the secluded life which circumstances and her
temperament made congenial. She looked upon outside affairs from a certain distance ; and though
Lewes's eager interest in all manner of contemporary
controversies kept her in touch with the more
thoughtful minds of the day, she had little opportunity for direct familiarity with the manners and
customs of society.

The year 1865 was marked by two new literary
ventures, in both of which Lewes took some part.
The *Pall Mall Gazette* was started at the beginning
of the year, and the first number of the *Fortnightly
Review*, of which Lewes was the first editor, came out
in the following May.   Both attracted many able
writers, and the adoption of signed articles by the
review introduced a novel practice in English journal-
ism.   George Eliot contributed a few articles to both,
and was interested in the attempt to raise the standard
of periodical writing. She was only distracted, however, for the moment from more serious work. The
notes in her diary on September 6, 1864: " I am
reading about Spain, and trying a drama on a subject
that has fascinated me — have written the prologue,
and am beginning the first act.   But I have little

hope of making anything satisfactory." By the end
of the year she had written three acts. On 21st
February 1865 she describes herself as "ill and very
miserable: George has taken my drama away from
me " — the consequence, obviously, and not the cause
of her misery. The drama was put aside for some
time, and by the end of March she had begun her next
novel, *Felix Holt*. It was finished in a little more than
a year. Smith, it seems, declined to give £5000 for
it — the sum presumably fixed by Lewes; but Blackwood accepted the terms, and she now returned to
him for the rest of her life, though without any breach
of friendship with Smith. The novel was written amid
the usual fits of depression, and with the same elaborate
care as its predecessors. "I finished writing," she
says, "after days and nights of throbbing and palpita-
tion — chiefly, I suppose, from a nervous excitement
which I was not strong enough to support well." She
had been painstaking in more ways than one. She
went through the *Times* of 1832–3 at the British
Museum in order to correct her childish memories
of the period. She is in "a horrible fidget" about
certain assumptions in the story. She wants especially
to have an answer to two questions: first, whether
after the Treaty of Amiens "the seizure and imprison-
ment of civilians was exceptional, and whether it was
continued throughout the war "; and secondly, whether
in 1833 a person sentenced to transportation without
hard labour might be set at large on his arrival in the
colony. The story again involved some complex legal
relations. She began, it seems, by reading Sugden,
but happily relieved herself from the need of getting up the law of real property by committing the

problem to Mr. Frederic Harrison. The right to an estate must be suddenly transferred to a young woman; but the ordinary novelist's device of a discovery that her birth was legitimate is not applicable. The change must be effected by the death of somebody who has himself no interest in the matter; and both the actual possessor and the person to whom the right passes must be left in ignorance that the title to the estate will be affected by the death. How this is brought about may be discovered from the story itself. Mr. Harrison's law is said, as we can well believe, to be perfectly correct. Probably the average reader will be quite content to take it as correct without consulting Sugden. Meanwhile, he is rather bored by the fear that unless he clearly understands both the law and the facts, he will lose something essential to the point of the story. When one reads Wilkie Collins or Gaboriau, one is content to have a secret carefully hidden, and bits of apparent irrelevance introduced, because the chief pleasure is to consist in guessing at the connection and admiring the ingenuity with which the fragments of the puzzle are to be pieced together at the end. But in a work of such serious intention as *Felix Holt*, the mystery is felt to be teasing, and we should be more really interested if we were taken into the author's confidence at once. The genuine artist ought to be above the "long-lost heir" trick or the complicated substitutes for the old-fashioned device.

This worrying perplexity which runs through the whole partly explains the inferiority of *Felix Holt* to its predecessors. But another change is more important. We have got back from Florence of the

Renaissance to the English midlands during the
Reform Bill agitation, and for that we may be thank-
ful.   But George Eliot is no longer drawing upon the
old memories of Griff.   She turns to account an election
riot which, we are told, she had seen in her schooldays
at Nuneaton; but she is thinking mainly of the
Coventry time.   Mrs. Poyser and her dairy have
vanished, and with them the old-world charm.   We
have no longer the peculiar glamour which invested
the former stories; the sense of looking at the little
world through the harmonising atmosphere of childish
memories and affections; or of becoming for the nonce
denizens of a social order, narrow enough in its
interests, but yet wholesome, kindly, and contented.
We have some of the old-fashioned country gentry
and parsons who fill the subordinate parts satisfac-
torily enough; but the principal interest is to be in
the county-town of Treby Magna, just waking to the
consciousness of the great political movement outside,
and with little enough that was romantic about its
lawyers, tradesmen, or manufacturers.   Canals and
coal-mines and a saline spring are beginning to rouse
it from its "old-fashioned, grazing, brewing, wool-
packing, cheese-loading life"; and the change only
seems to reveal thoroughly prosaic, not to say vulgar
and stupefying characteristics.   There is no suggestion
of any lingering fondness for an order which is essentially mean as well as obsolete.   Naturally, therefore,
we are expected to sympathise with Felix Holt the
Radical, who is trying to stir up this stagnant pool.

George Eliot, in fact, is now occupied with the
problem which is already suggested by her previous
works.   She had strong conservative tendencies, and

a dislike for violent and one-sided reforms.   Hitherto
she had emphasised her sympathy for the higher
purposes and aspirations which were hidden under the
commonplace and even superstitious modes of life and
thought.   But, after all, she is also fully convinced that
intellectual progress and a larger culture are essential
and important; and her tenderness for the past must
not be allowed to sanction reactionary tendencies.
Romola has already been troubled by the problem
in one phase, and it is now to be presented to us in
various shapes.   Young men or women, troubled
with active intellects, have to rouse from their comfortable slumbers and to provide themselves with an
ideal; they will become missionaries of a new creed,
and have the usual difficulties of the position.   If
they quarrel with the past too contemptuously, they
may become mere visionary fanatics; and if too much
inclined to compromise, they may sacrifice their aspirations and yield to the benumbing influence of
respectability.   The ordinary novelist is content with
telling us how a young couple contrive to come together without bothering themselves at all about the
Universe or their relation to the general progress of
humanity.   George Eliot, though her interests in
philosophical questions may be a little too intrusive,
may still deserve gratitude for introducing a new
motive, and showing us the fate of young people affected
by the unusual weakness of preoccupation with ideals.

Felix Holt represents an experiment upon this
theme.   He is an admirable but, I fear it must be
admitted, a far from satisfactory representative of his
breed.   He is a radical of the days of 1832; and
George Eliot, as we have seen, had been refreshing her

memories of that period by reading the old newspapers, and had been surprised by the strength of the
language about " bloated pluralists " and so forth.
We should naturally have expected that the eloquence
of Felix Holt would have reflected the same sentiment.
He is a working man, and had managed to be a student
at Glasgow, where there was plenty of good fiery
radicalism ; and, in fact, he starts with a hearty contempt for the upper classes, and thinks a Whig no
better than a Tory in disguise. Such a man might
swear by Cobbett or by Owen, and would probably
take his religious views from Paine's *Age of Reason*.
He would be of the stuff of which the Chartists were
soon to be made ; would believe that the millennium
was to be introduced by the famous six points ; and
would certainly favour the abolition of the monarchy
and the House of Lords and the confiscation of Church
property. George Eliot might have shown us how
such doctrines were a natural, though it might be, a
too precipitate outcome of really philanthropic and
generous feelings in a man of the day. Ebenezer
Elliott, the " Tyrtæus " of the Anti-Corn Law movement, and Thomas Cooper, the Chartist poet, were
men in Felix Holt's position, who shared his vehemence and came to be alienated from the violent
section of their allies. Felix Holt, however, has to be
a model young man, and therefore he sees from the
first the errors of contemporary zealots. When a
self-styled radical orator addresses a public meeting
and demands "universal suffrage," and the other points
of the Charter, Felix appeals to reason. Systems of
suffrage and the rest, he tells the mob, are engines :
the force that is to work them must come from men's

passions. No scheme will do good, therefore, unless the power behind it takes a right direction. The "steam that is to work the engines" is public opinion, that is, "the ruling belief in society about what is right and what is wrong, what is honourable and what is shameful." Nothing, therefore, is to be expected from a party which sanctions bribery and corruption. When Felix makes a personal application of this lofty doctrine by pointing out that the agent of his own party is an embodiment of corruption, he naturally produces loud cheers; but the doctrine itself, however philosophical, would hardly have pleased his audience. Soon after the appearance of the novel George Eliot published in *Blackwood* "An Address to Working Men, by Felix Holt," which enforces the same moral. It may be, as I believe myself, that her principle is a very sound one. Still one perceives that it is a principle which will be much more easily accepted by readers of *Blackwood's Magazine* than by the "working man" to whom it is ostensibly addressed. He will only see that it is a highly convenient argument for putting off all reform. With that, however, I am not concerned. The effect in the novel is to take the sting out of the hero. He is too reasonable for his part. He is introduced as a redhot radical, and shows it by extreme rudeness to Esther, whom he suspects of fine-ladyism. Esther, being an admirable young woman, comes to see that he is right, and even that there is something complimentary in his exasperation against her. I should have liked him better if he had been exasperated to rudeness against his political enemies, and shown his sound judgment by gentle treatment of the trifling petulance of a pretty girl.

No doubt, Felix is an honourable man, for he refuses to live upon a quack medicine or to look leniently at bribery when it is on his own side. But there is a painful excess of sound judgment about him. He gets into prison, not for leading a mob, but for trying to divert them from plunder by actions which are mis-understood. He is very inferior to Alton Locke, who gets into prison for a similar performance. The im-petuosity and vehemence only comes out in his rude-ness to Esther and plain speaking to her adopted father; and in trying to make him an ideal of wisdom, George Eliot only succeeds in making him unfit for his part.

If, therefore, we are to accept the indication given by the title, and suppose that Felix Holt is to be the focus of interest, the novel, I think, fails of its effect. We no more see the rough, thorough-going radical, stung to fury by pauperism and the slavery of children in factories, and sharing the zeal and the illusions of Jacobins, than we saw the true spirit of the Renaissance in *Romola*. Mr. Felix Holt would have been quite in his place at Toynbee Hall; but is much too cold-blooded for the time when revolution and confiscation were really in the air. Perhaps this indicates the want of masculine fibre in George Eliot and the deficient sym-pathy with rough popular passions which makes us feel that he represents the afterthought of the judicious sociologist and not the man of flesh and blood who was the product of the actual conditions. Anyhow, the novel appears to be regarded as her least interesting. There are undoubtedly many charming scenes. One would be disposed to think that Rufus Lyon, the old dissenting minister, was more of a contemporary of

Baxter than could have been possible at the time; but
one cannot say confidently what survivals of the type
there may have been at Coventry, and his simplicity
and pedantry and power of emphasising the highest
elements in the creed of his sect show the art of a
skilled humorist. Esther, too, with her naïve appreciation of the charms of a luxurious life, is too good for
Felix. But the really strongest part of the novel is
old Mrs. Transome, brooding over her sorrows, and
dwelling remorsefully upon her error in the past.
" If she had only been more haggard and less majestic,
those who had glimpses of her outward life might
have said that she was a griping harridan with a
tongue like a razor. No one said exactly that; but
they never said anything like the full truth about her,
or divined what was hidden under her outward life
— a woman's keen sensibility and dread, which lay
screened behind all her petty habits and narrow
notions as some quivering thing with eyes and throbbing heart may lie crouching behind withered rubbish.
The sensibility and dread had palpitated all the faster
in the prospect of her son's return; and now that she
had seen him, she said to herself in her bitter way,
'It is a lucky cub that escapes skinning. The best
happiness I shall ever know will be to escape the worst
misery.'" That is one of the striking passages in
which George Eliot shows her vivid insight into
certain moods and characters. Mrs. Transome, I confess, interests me so much that I should have liked to
know a little more about that early intrigue which has
soured her, and how she came to be fascinated by the
old lover, who by the time at which the book opens
has shown his inferior nature and uses the old memories

to insult her. I could willingly have spared, in order
to make room for a little more of the family scandal,
some of the elaborate legal complications, and of
Mr. Felix Holt's clumsy performances as a prophet
of social reform.

CHAPTER XI

FELIX HOLT, as we have seen, had been taken up at a time when she was in despair of finishing a drama which Lewes for once did not altogether approve. She had written three or four acts, and on reading the old work again "found it impossible to abandon it." The conceptions moved her deeply, and had "never been wrought out before." Still it required entire recasting. Some of her views at the time are given in an interesting letter to Mr. Frederic Harrison (15th August 1866). He had, it seems, proposed some theme for her consideration. "That," she says, "is a tremendously difficult problem which you have laid before me; and I think you see its difficulties, though they can hardly press on you as they do on me, who have gone through again and again the severe effort of trying to make certain ideas thoroughly incarnate, as if they had revealed themselves to me just in the flesh, and not in the spirit. I think æsthetic teaching is the highest of all teaching, because it deals with life in its highest complexity; but if it ceases to be purely æsthetic, if it lapses anywhere from the picture to the diagram, it becomes the most offensive of all teaching." She proceeds to point out the "agonising labour to an English-fed imagination to make out a sufficiently real background for the desired picture — to get breathing individual forms and group them in the needful relations, so that the presentation will lay hold on the emotions as human experience — will, as you say, ' flash ' conviction on the world by means of aroused sympathy." She recalls the " unspeakable pains " involved in the preparation of *Romola* and the acquisition of the necessary Italian " idiom." The problem suggested by Mr. Harrison — its precise nature is not told — would, she thinks, be one of " tenfold arduousness." The statement shows George Eliot's perception of the real difficulty. " Ideas " may be seen " in the flesh" or " in the spirit": that is, I take it, as the abstract formulæ of philosophy or as the concrete visions of poetry. The question is whether the writer who starts from the abstract can by industrious study so incarnate his ideas that they may be as vivid and real as if he had started from the opposite point of view. " Enough ! " one is induced to say, as Rasselas says to Imlac, " thou hast convinced me that no human being" (and no philosopher) " can ever be a poet." No deliberate absorption of imagery can ever make up for the direct spontaneous intuition, and a task which involves " agonising labour " is likely enough to result in painful reading. Why undertake it ?

George Eliot, however, thought differently, and attempted to achieve this difficult task in the *Spanish Gypsy*. She is soon " swimming in Spanish history and literature," and on 15th October 1866 begins the recasting. Early in 1867 she visited Spain to get up the local colouring, and after many changes the poem was at last finished on 29th April 1868. Lewes was in an " unprecedented state of delight," and especially

pleased with the "variety" of the work, because he
had persuaded her to put it aside "on the ground of
monotony." The book, though the sale was considerable, roused some hostile criticism at the time, and
has not convinced even her warmest admirers that she
was in her proper place as a poet. She left a note
upon its history which is interesting, as giving her own
defence against the obvious reasons for dissatisfaction,
and as illustrating her general position. The subject,
it seems, was originally suggested by a picture of the
Annunciation, ascribed to Titian in the Scuola di san
Rocco at Venice. It embodied, she thought, a "great
dramatic motive." A maiden, "full of young hope,"
and about to share in the ordinary lot of womanhood,
is suddenly made aware that she is to fulfil a great
destiny, and to have a terribly different experience.
"Here," she thought, "is a subject grander than that
of Iphigenia, and it has never been used." She
then tried to find an appropriate embodiment, and
could think of nothing except the moment of Spanish
history when the struggle with the Moors was attain-
ing its climax. She could not make use of Moors
and Jews, because the "facts of their history were
too conspicuously opposed to the working out of
my catastrophe." Facts have that awkward habit.
She thought, however (though the point is surely
doubtful), that this objection did not apply to the
Gypsies. The subject, as she meditated, became
"more and more pregnant." It might be "a symbol
of the part which is played by hereditary conditions
in the largest sense, and of the fact that what we
call duty is entirely made up of such conditions."
Tragedy consists in the "terrible difficulty of adjust-

ing our individual needs to the dire necessity of our lot," in which, of course, the lives of our fellow-creatures are involved. The great Greek tragedies often turn upon such a conflict between the inherited Nemesis and the individual whom it crushes. *Othello* becomes a " most pathetic tragedy " instead of a simple story of jealousy, on account " of the hereditary conditions of Othello's lot " — a point surely not much considered by Shakespeare. We may grant, however, that a tragedy may thus show the individual giving way to the general. It cannot explain why the conflict should arise, but it sets forth the pathetic consequences. In the *Spanish Gypsy* the action represents the loving and sympathetic instincts which are converted into " piety, *i.e.* loving, willing submission and heroic Promethean effort towards high possibilities." Certain remarks upon ethical doctrines are apparently meant to show that such instincts cannot be governed by " rational reflection," and therefore may at once arouse sympathy and lead to terrible scrapes. There are, however, two " consolatory elements " woven into the very warp of the poem : " (1) The importance of individual deeds; (2) the all-sufficiency of the soul's passions in determining sympathetic action." I mention these elements, as George Eliot attaches so much importance to them, though I confess that they do not much console me. One other remark is noteworthy. It might, she says, be " a reasonable ground of objection against the whole structure of the *Spanish Gypsy* if it were shown that the action is outrageously impossible — lying outside all that can be congruously conceived of human actions. It is *not* a reasonable ground of objection

M

that they would have done better to act otherwise, any more than it is a reasonable objection against the *Iphigenia* that Agamemnon would have done better not to sacrifice his daughter."

It is plain that if the *Spanish Gypsy* failed to succeed, it was not for want of careful consideration of æsthetic principles. Moreover, without following this excursion into theories, we may, I think, take one result for granted. Undoubtedly, the conflict between "the individual" and "the general," or, say, between the duties which a human being owes to his own friends and family, and those which he owes to his country or his gods, may be an admirable theme for tragedy. Fedalma, George Eliot's heroine, is distracted between her love for her destined bridegroom and her sense of duty to the race from which she sprang. Nobody will deny that such a struggle presents an interesting and worthy theme. The difficulty comes afterwards. Why did George Eliot suppose that the only fitting historical embodiment was at "a particular period of Spanish history"? This seems to involve a singular leap in the logic. It is especially noticeable in a writer who has insisted that the highest motives may be found under commonplace outsides; that country parsons and farmers may have the "root of the matter" in them; and that even the passions which inspired the Greek tragedies may be shown at work in the breast of an eight years' old girl. "Heredity" has been annexed of late years by "realistic" novelists; but, in any case, the struggle between loyalty to our race or family instincts, and the wider forces of evolution, might be illustrated from transactions less obscure than the struggle in the Spain of the fifteenth

century. A hopeful young English maiden of the
nineteenth may be, called upon to choose between
making a respectable marriage and devoting herself to
some impracticable ideal with tragical, if perhaps also
comic, results. Why place the heroine among conditions so hard to imagine?

One consequence of George Eliot's choice of this
romantic setting for her characters is obvious. In
romance we have to take leave of common sense.
That is an easy sacrifice to make on some occasions.
Children, even grown-up children, may delight in fairy
tales and the Arabian Nights, though they get into a
region where the impossible is the order of the day
and morality ceases to be binding. Poetically-minded
people can still take some pleasure, I believe, in the
old romances, and find in Spenser's *Faerie Queene* not
only a delightful series of pictures, but poetry informed
with a lofty spirit of chivalry. But in the *Spanish
Gypsy* we cannot get so far from downright historical
fact. Our ethical sentiment is to be seriously interested, and conviction is to be "flashed" upon us by
aroused sympathy. Now, to sympathise to any purpose
we must understand. We must be able to appreciate
the difficulty of the position and the severity of the
ordeal. Here, however, we are terribly at a loss. The
critical scene of the *Spanish Gypsy* is the first interview between Fedalma and Zarca. Fedalma has been
brought up from her earliest infancy as a Catholic and
a Spaniard. She has only seen the gypsies as a band
of prisoners brought through the town in chains. She
is on the eve of marriage to a typical Spanish noble,
with whom she is passionately in love. To her enters
abruptly one of the gypsies. He explains without loss

of time that he is her father; that he is about to be the
Moses or Mahomet of a gypsy nation in Africa; and
orders her to give up her country, her religion, and
her lover to join him in this hopeful enterprise. She
is, of course, a good deal put out, and explains some
obvious objections; but after exchanging some para-
graphs of blank verse, she walks off with her parent,
leaving a short note to inform her lover that she can
have nothing more to do with him. Admit the least
touch of common sense, and the situation is surely, in
George Eliot's words, " outrageously impossible." We
know enough of the gypsies of history to perceive that
Zarca behaved like a lunatic. We may try to escape
by dropping history and regarding " Spain," like
Shakespeare's Bohemia, as a phrase belonging to
the geography of simple romance. But, then, the
whole story becomes too unreal to appeal to our
sympathies. We are able to accept the position of
Iphigenia, to which George Eliot appeals, as treated by
Euripides, or even by Racine, and for the moment
take for granted that the human sacrifice is a reasonable mode of conduct. That assumption once made, the
position becomes clear. The father is bound to kill
the daughter, because, as we know, the gods will be
pleased. But the difficulty of the Spanish Gypsy is
that if we try, as George Eliot tried, to imagine
the actual state of things, the dilemma is absurd;
and if we substitute a world of pure fancy, everything becomes arbitrary. We do not see why
the daughter is bound to act like a lunatic. She
informs us, of course, that she is deeply affected, but
we cannot perceive that her motives are reasonable
and intelligible. Considered from the ethical side,

the objection seems to be fatal.   Dr. Congreve, an
adequate authority, said that it was a "mass of
positivism."   The meaning, if an outsider may venture
a guess, seems to be that the positivist insists upon a
view of duty as corresponding to the vital instincts of
the "social organism"; the identification of the individual with the body of which he is the product, and
the constituent and consequent readiness to sacrifice
life and happiness to the interest of the community
into which he is born.   This doctrine was already
preached, though in an imperfect form, by Savonarola to
Romola, and becomes prominent in the *Spanish Gypsy.*
Now one may accept the principle as true and valuable,
and yet regard the story as a *reductio ad absurdum* of
some applications.   Fedalma, in her first interview with
Zarca, exclaims —

> " Father, my soul is not too base to ring
>   At touch of your great thoughts ; nay, in my blood
>   There streams the sense unspeakable of kind,
>   As leopard feels at ease with leopard."

The human being should have higher instincts than
the leopard.   Fedalma, however, is gradually led to
admit the supreme force of this appeal.   She will not
be "half-hearted."

> "I will seek nothing but to shun base joy.
>   The saints were cowards who stood by to see
>   Christ crucified : they should have flung themselves
>   Upon the Roman spears, and died in vain —
>   The grandest death, to die in vain — for love,
>   Greater than sways the forces of the world !
>   That death shall be my bridegroom.   I will wed
>   The curse that blights my people."

Of course, the young lady is excited.   She is in the
state of mind in which irrationality is a recommenda-

tion. Death surely is made grand by the grandeur of the purpose, not by the futility of the means. Surely the death of the early Christians and their master would not be grander if we held that their zeal was wasted on an ideal as absurd as Fedalma's. Her doctrine, stated in cold blood, seems to be that our principles are to be determined by the physical fact of ancestry. The discovery that my father was a Saxon or a Celt might perhaps be allowed to affect my sympathies, but surely should not change my views of home-rule. In an interval of common sense Fedalma suggests that she will marry and persuade her husband to protect the gypsies. Nobody could object to that; but to throw overboard all other ties on the simple ground of descent, and adopt the most preposterous schemes of the vagabonds to whom you are related, seems to be very bad morality whatever may be its affinity to positivism.

The error seems to be precisely that George Eliot was hopelessly trammelled by the conditions which she had accepted. She could not get her abstract principle to become "incarnate" in facts. She falls into a hopeless entanglement. The facts become absurd, and the principle has to be distorted. It may still be asked whether, in spite of such views, the *Spanish Gypsy* is not a great poem. *Paradise Lost* is a masterpiece poetically, though its theology is grotesque and its proposed justification of Providence an admitted failure. Can we say anything of the kind on behalf of the *Spanish Gypsy* ? It may clearly be said that it certainly shows a powerful intellect stored with noble sentiment and impelled to utter great thoughts. It illustrates curiously the union observed by Lewes of

great diffidence with great ambition. She aims at
the highest mark, though at any given moment she
is despondent of achievement. She adopted the title
of the poem, she says, because it recalled the old
dramatists, with whom she thought she had "more
cousinship than with recent poets." [1]   It seems to have
been first written in the dramatic form ; though, as
finished, it became a set of scenes interspersed with
digressions into epic poetry. The passages which
would be represented in the regular drama by stage
directions are expanded into descriptive writing or
into psychological disquisitions intended to introduce
us to the characters. The old dramatists, to whom
she refers, might give a precedent for introducing a
good many sententious remarks upon human life
which have no very direct relation to the story ;
but, in truth, she reminds us rather of "Philip van
Artevelde" and other modern plays not intended for
the stage; and if we complain that the book tried by
dramatic tests becomes languid, it may be replied that
we have had fair notice that it belongs to a different
genus and should be judged from the author's point
of view. This, however, does not answer the ordinary
objection that, after all, it is not poetry ; or does not
decisively cross the indefinable but essential line which
divides true poetry from the highest rhetoric. Here
and there is a fine phrase, as in the opening passage
about —

> "Broad-breasted Spain, leaning with equal love
> On the Mid Sea that moans with memories,
> And on the untravelled Ocean's restless tides."

---

[1] Middleton's *Spanish Gipsie* was acted about 1621.

Or a few lines later —

> " What times are little ?   To the sentinel
>   That hour is regal when he mounts on guard."

Passages often sound exactly like poetry; and yet, even her admirers admit that they seldom, if ever, have the genuine ring.   They do not satisfy the old criterion that nothing can be poetry, in the full sense, of which we are disposed to say that it would be as good in prose.   The lyrics which are interspersed are palpable if clever imitations of the genuine thing.   Perhaps it was simply that George Eliot had not one essential gift — the exquisite sense for the value of words which may transmute even common thought into poetry. Even her prose, indeed, though often admirable, some-times becomes heavy, and gives the impression that instead of finding the right word she is accumulating more or less complicated approximations.   Then one might inquire whether, after all, the problem of " in-carnating " the abstract idea, if not really impracticable from the beginning, was suited to her powers.   The dramatic form especially demands the intuitive instead of the discursive attitude of mind, and the vivid " presentation " of concrete men and women instead of the thoughtful analysis of their character.   Might she not succeed by accepting the conditions frankly, and attempting, in spite of its bad name, an avowedly " philosophical form " ?   She loved Wordsworth well enough to forgive his admitted shortcomings; and if the *Excursion* is undeniably dull, it is still a work which, in spite of all critical condemnations, has pro-foundly impressed the spiritual development of many eminent persons.

George Eliot was in fact led to try various poetical experiments. A volume of poems published in 1874 contained the "Legend of Jubal," begun in 1869, "How Lisa loved the King" (from Boccaccio), "Agatha," "Armgart," and "A College Breakfast Party," which were written in the same period. That they all show great literary ability is undeniable, though it is still doubtful whether they show more. The "College Breakfast," with its downright plunge into metaphysics, set forth with an abundant display of metaphor and illustration, is a singular exhibition of (as I must think) misapplied ingenuity; and chiefly interesting to people who may wish to know George Eliot's judgment of Hegelianism, æstheticism, and positivism. The most remarkable, however, is the short poem called "O may I join the choir invisible." It has been accepted by many who sympathise with her religious views. The invisible choir is formed of those "immortal dead who live again in minds made better by their presence." So to live, we are told, "is heaven." The generous natures have set their example before us, and our "rarer, better, truer self" finds in them a help to harmonise discordant impulses, and seek a loftier ideal.

> " The better self shall live till human Time
>   Shall fold its eyelids, and the human sky
>   Be gathered like a scroll within the tomb
>   Unread for ever.
>   This is life to come
>   Which martyred men have made more glorious
>   For us who strive to follow.   May I reach
>   That purest heaven, be to other souls
>   The cup of strength in some great agony,

> Enkindle generous ardour, feed pure love,
> Beget the smiles that have no cruelty —
> Be the sweet presence of a good diffused,
> And in diffusion ever more intense.
> So shall I join the choir invisible
> Whose music is the gladness of the world."

To appreciate the sacred poetry of any church, one ought to be an orthodox member; and, to many people, of course, immortality thus understood seems to be rather a mockery. It would be better, they think, to admit frankly that immortality is a figment. Even they may agree that the aspiration is lofty and eloquently expressed. Reflections upon a similar theme inspire two other poems. Armgart is a *prima donna*, rejoicing in the overpowering success of her first appearance, who suddenly loses her voice by a sudden attack of throat disease; and has to reconcile herself to the abandonment of her hopes, and to becoming part of the choir inaudible. " Jubal " — which seems to me to be the nearest approach to genuine poetry — is the story of the patriarch who invented music. He leaves his tribe for a journey which, as he has the prediluvian longevity, is protracted for an indefinite time, and when he returns finds that people have got out of the habit of living for centuries. The descendants of his contemporaries are celebrating a feast in honour of the inventor of music; and, when he innocently observes that he is the person in question, he is pooh-poohed without further inquiry. As he lies down to die his Past appears to him, and explains that he should be content with having bestowed the great gift upon mankind.

" Thy limbs shall lie dark, tombless on the sod,
   Because thou shinest in man's soul, a God,
   Who found and gave new passion and new joy
   That nought but earth's destruction can destroy."

The excellent R. H. Hutton was offended by the
doctrine of this poem, especially by the apparent
implication that death is, on the whole, a good thing,
because it induced a race, which had taken things too
easily as long as they fancied that they had an indefinite time before them, to rouse themselves and
invent musical as well as other instruments. The
logic indeed — if really intended — does not appear to
be very cogent. The moral that, as we have got to die,
we should be content with the consciousness of having
played our part, without expecting reward or bothering
ourselves about posthumous fame, is more to the purpose. Jubal, who happily lived in a purely legend-
ary region, does not come into conflict with historical
facts like Fedalma, and may be taken as a satisfactory
poetical symbol of a characteristic mood, suggested by
the old thought of mortality and oblivion. I cannot,
indeed, believe that George Eliot achieved a permanent position in English poetry: she is a remarkable, I suppose unique, case, of a writer taking to
poetry at the ripe age of forty-four, by which the
majority of poets have done their best work. Perhaps
that suggests that the impulse was acquired rather
than innate, and more likely to succeed in impressing
reflective and melancholy minds than in vivid presentation of concrete images.

CHAPTER XII

MIDDLEMARCH

THE poetic impulse seems to have decayed soon after the *Spanish Gypsy*, as George Eliot gradually became absorbed in another novel. On 1st January 1869 she notes that she has projected a novel, to be called *Middlemarch*, besides a " long poem on Timoleon," of which we hear nothing more. *Middlemarch* at first made slow progress. She began the " Vincy and Featherstone parts " in August. It is not till December 1870 that she is beginning a story to be called " Miss Brooke," without any very serious intention " of carrying it out lengthily." It became amalgamated with the other story. George Eliot appears to have suffered even more than usual from ill-health and despondency during the composition, and was troubled at times by the difficulty of bringing a superabundant variety of motives into artistic unity. The book was published on a new plan, coming out in eight parts — the first on 1st December 1871, and the last in December 1872. *Middlemarch*, she says, was received with as much enthusiasm as any of her former books, not even excepting *Adam Bede*. Its commercial success is proved by the fact that she made more by it than by *Romola*. Nearly 25,000 copies had been sold before the end of 1875. George Eliot was now admittedly the first living

novelist.   Thackeray and Dickens were both dead,
and no survivor of her generation could be counted
as a rival.   When a writer's fame is once established,
the reception of his books is apt to be disproportion-
ately favourable.   They are read not only by genuine
admirers, but by all who know that they ought to
admire.   The immediate success of *Middlemarch* may
have been proportioned rather to the author's reputation than to its intrinsic merits.   It certainly lacks
the peculiar charm of the early work, and one understands why the *Spectator* should have been led to say
that George Eliot was "the most melancholy of
authors."   The conclusion was apparently softened to
meet this objection.   There is not much downright
tragedy, but the general impression is unmistakably
sad.   This, however, does not prevent *Middlemarch*
from having, in some ways, even a stronger interest
than its companions.   George Eliot was now over
fifty, and the book represents the general tone of her
reflection upon life and human nature.   By that age
most people have had some rather unpleasant aspects
of life pretty strongly forced upon their attention ; and
George Eliot, though she made it a principle to take
things cheerfully, had never had much of the buoyancy
which generates optimism.   She was not, she used to
say, either an optimist or a pessimist, but a "meliorist,"
—a believer that the world could be improved, and was
perhaps slowly improving, though with a very strong
conviction that the obstacles were enormous and the
immediate outlook not specially bright.   Some people,
it seems, attributed her sadness to her creed, though I
fancy that, in such matters, creed has much less to do
with the matter than temperament.   So sensitive a

woman, working so conscientiously and with so many
misgivings, could hardly make her imaginary world a
cheerful place of residence. *Middlemarch* is primarily
a portrait of the circles which had been most familiar
to her in youth, and its second title is " a study of
provincial life."   Provincial life, however, is to ex-
emplify the results of a wider survey of contemporary
society.   One peculiarity of the book is appropriate
to this scheme.   It is not a story, but a combination
of at least three stories — the love affairs of Dorothea
and Casaubon, of Rosamond Vincy and Lydgate, and
of Mary Garth and Fred Vincy, which again are interwoven with the story of Bulstrode.   The various
actions get mixed together as they would naturally
do in a country town.   Modern English novelists
seem to have made up their mind that this kind of
mixture is contrary to the rules of art.   I am content
to say that I used to find some old novels written on
that plan very interesting.   It is tiresome, of course,
if a reader is to think only of the development of the
plot.   But when the purpose is to get a general picture
of the manners and customs of a certain social stratum,
and we are to be interested in all the complex play of
character and the opinions of neighbours, the method
is appropriate to the design.   The individuals are
shown as involved in the network of surrounding
interests which affects their development.   *Middlemarch* gives us George Eliot's most characteristic view
of such matters.   It is her answer to the question,
What on the whole is your judgment of commonplace
English life? for " provincialism " is not really confined
to the provinces.   Without trying to put the answer
into a single formula, and it would be very unjust to

her to assume that such a formula was intended, I may note one leading doctrine : —

"An eminent philosopher among my friends," she says, with a characteristically scientific illustration, "who can dignify even your ugly furniture by lifting it into the serene light of science, has shown me this pregnant little fact.   Your pier-glass, an extensive surface of polished steel made to be rubbed by a housemaid, will be minutely and multitudinously scratched in all directions ; but place now against it a lighted candle as a centre of illumination, and the scratches will seem to arrange themselves in a fine series of concentric circles round that little sun.   It is demonstrable that the scratches are going everywhere impartially, and it is only your candle which produces the flattering illusion of a concentric arrangement, its light falling into an exclusive optical selection.   These things are a parable" — showing the effect of egoism.   It may also represent the effect of a novelist's mental preoccupation.   Many different views of human society may be equally true to fact ; but the writer, who has a particular "candle," in the shape of a favourite principle, produces a spontaneous unity by its application to the varying cases presented.   The personages who carry out the various plots of *Middlemarch* may be, as I think they are, very lifelike portraits of real life, but they are seen from a particular point of view.   The "prelude" gives the keynote.   We are asked to remember the childish adventure of Saint Theresa setting out to seek martyrdom in the country of the Moors.   Her "passionate, ideal nature demanded an epic life . . . some object which would reconcile self-despair with the rapturous consciousness of life

beyond self. . . . She ultimately found her epos in
the reform of a religious order." There are later-born
Theresas, who had "no epic life with a constant
unfolding of far-resonant action." They have had to
work amid "dim lights and tangled circumstances";
they have been "helped by no coherent social faith
and ardour which could perform the function of
knowledge for the ardently thrilling soul." They
have blundered accordingly; but "here and there is
born a Saint Theresa, foundress of nothing, whose
loving heart-beats and sobs after an unattained goodness tremble off, and are dispersed among hindrances,
instead of centring on some long recognisable deed."
We are to see how such a nature manifests itself — no
longer in the remote regions of arbitrary fancy, but in
the commonplace atmosphere of a modern English
town. In Maggie Tulliver and in Felix Holt we have
already had the struggle for an ideal; but in *Middlemarch* there is a fuller picture of the element of
stupidity and insensibility which is apt to clog the
wings of aspiration. The Dodsons, among whom
Maggie is placed, belong to the stratum of sheer
bovine indifference. They are not only without
ideas, but it has never occurred to them that such
things exist. In *Middlemarch* we consider the higher
stratum, which reads newspapers and supports the
Society for the Diffusion of Useful Knowledge, and
whose notions constitute what is called enlightened
public opinion. The typical representative of what it
calls its mind is Mr. Brooke, who can talk about Sir
Humphry Davy, and Wordsworth, and Italian art,
and has a delightful facility in handling the small
change of conversation which has ceased to possess

any intrinsic value. Even his neighbours can see that he is a fatuous humbug, and do not care to veil their blunt common sense by fine phrases. But he discharges the functions of the Greek chorus with a boundless supply of the platitudes which represent an indistinct foreboding of the existence of an intellectual world.

Dorothea, brought up with Mr. Brooke in place of a parent, is to be a Theresa struggling under " dim lights and entangled circumstances." She is related, of course, both to Maggie and to Romola, though she is not in danger of absolute asphyxiation in a dense bucolic atmosphere, or of martyrdom in the violent struggles of hostile creeds. Her danger is rather that of being too easily acclimatised in a comfortable state of things, where there is sufficient cultivation and no particular demand for St. Theresas. She attracts us by her perfect straightforwardness and simplicity, though we are afraid that she has even a slight touch of stupidity. We fancy that she might find satisfaction, like other young ladies, in looking after schools and the unhealthy cottages on her uncle's estate. Still, she has a real loftiness of character, and a disposition to take things seriously, which make her more or less sensible of the limitations of her circle. She has vague religious aspirations, looks down upon the excellent country gentleman, Sir James Chettam, and fancies that she would like to marry the judicious Hooker, or Milton in his blindness. We can understand, and even pardon her, when she takes the pedant Casaubon at his own valuation, and sees in him " a living Bossuet, whose work would reconcile complete knowledge with devoted piety, a modern Augustine who united the glories of doctor and saint."

N

Dorothea's misguided adoration is, I think, very natural, but it is undeniably painful, and many readers protested. The point is curious. George Eliot declared that she had lived in much sympathy with Casaubon's life, and was especially gratified when some one saw the pathos of his career. No doubt there is a pathos in devotion to an entirely mistaken ideal. To spend a life in researches, all thrown away from ignorance of what has been done, is a melancholy fate. One secret of Casaubon's blunder was explained to his wife during the honeymoon. He had not — as Ladislaw pointed out — read the Germans, and was therefore groping through a wood with a pocket compass where they had made carriage roads. But suppose that he had read the last authorities? Would that have really mended matters? A deeper objection is visible even to his own circle. Solid Sir James Chettam remarks that he is a man "with no good red blood in his body," and Ladislaw curses him for "a cursed white-blooded pedantic coxcomb." Their judgment is confirmed by all that we hear of him. He marries, we are told, because he wants "female tendance for his declining years. Hence he determined to abandon himself to the stream of feeling, and perhaps was surprised to find what an exceedingly shallow rill it was." His petty jealousy and steady snubbing of his wife is all in character. Now we can pity a man for making a blunder, and perhaps, in some sense, we ought to "pity" him for having neither heart nor passion. But that is a kind of pity which is not akin to love. Dorothea's mistake was not that she married a man who had not read German, but that she married a stick instead of a man. The story, the more

fully we accept its truthfulness, becomes the more of
a satire against young ladies who aim at lofty ideals.
It implies a capacity for being imposed upon by a
mere outside shell of pretence. Then we have to ask
whether things are made better by her subsequent
marriage to Ladislaw? That equally offended some
readers, as George Eliot complained. Ladislaw is
almost obtrusively a favourite with his creator. He is
called "Will" for the sake of endearment; and we
are to understand him as so charming that Dorothea's
ability to keep him at a distance gives the most striking
proof of her strong sense of wifely duty. Yet Ladislaw is scarcely more attractive to most masculine readers than the dandified Stephen Guest. He is a dabbler
in art and literature; a small journalist, ready to
accept employment from silly Mr. Brooke, and apparently liking to lie on a rug in the houses of his
friends and flirt with their pretty wives. He certainly
shows indifference to money, and behaves himself
correctly to Dorothea, though he has fallen in love
with her on her honeymoon. He is no doubt an
amiable Bohemian, for some of whose peculiarities
it would be easy to suggest a living original, and
we can believe that Dorothea was quite content with
her lot. But that seems to imply that a Theresa
of our days has to be content with suckling fools and
chronicling small beer. We are told, indeed, that
Ladislaw became a reformer — apparently a "philosophical radical" — and even had the good luck to be
returned by a constituency who paid his expenses.
George Eliot ought to know; but I cannot believe in
this conclusion. Ladislaw, I am convinced, became
a brilliant journalist who could write smartly about

everything, but who had not the moral force to be a
leader in thought or action. I should be the last
person to deny that a journalist may lead an honourable and useful life, but I cannot think the profession
congenial to a lofty devotion to ideals. Dorothea was
content with giving him " wifely help "; asking his
friends to dinner, one supposes, and copying his ill-
written manuscripts. Many lamented that " so rare a
creature should be absorbed into the life of another,"
though no one could point out exactly what she ought
to have done. That is just the pity of it. There was
nothing for her to do; and I can only comfort myself
by reflecting that, after all, she had a dash of stupidity, and that more successful Theresas may do a
good deal of mischief.

The next pair of lovers gives a less ambiguous
moral. Lydgate, we are told, though we scarcely see
it, was a man of great energy, with a high purpose.
His ideal is shown by his ambition to be a leader in
medical science. In contrast to Casaubon, he is
thoroughly familiar with the latest authorities, and has
a capacity for really falling in love. Unfortunately,
Rosamond Vincy is a model of one of the forms of
stupidity against which the gods fight in vain. Being
utterly incapable of even understanding her husband's
aspirations, fixing her mind on the vulgar kind of
success, and having the strength of will which comes
from an absolute limitation to one aim, she is a most
effective torpedo, and paralyses all Lydgate's energies.
He is entangled in money difficulties; gives up his
aspirations; sinks into a merely popular physician,
and is sentenced to die early of diphtheria. A really
strong man, such as Lydgate is supposed to be, might

perhaps have made a better fight against the temptation and escaped that slavery to a pretty woman which
seems to have impressed George Eliot as the great
danger to the other sex. But she never, I think,
showed more power than in this painful history. The
skill with which Lydgate's gradual abandonment of
his lofty aims is worked out without making him
simply contemptible, forces us to recognise the
truthfulness of the conception. It is an inimitable
study of such a fascination as the snake is supposed to
exert upon the bird : the slow reluctant surrender, step
by step, of the higher to the lower nature, in consequence of weakness which is at least perfectly intelligible. George Eliot's "psychological analysis" is
here at its best; if it is not surpassed by the power
shown in Bulstrode. Bulstrode, too, has an ideal of a
kind; only it is the vulgar ideal which is suggested by
a low form of religion. George Eliot shows the ugly
side of the beliefs in which she had more frequently
emphasised the purer elements. But she still judges
without bitterness; and gives, perhaps, the most satisfactory portrait of the hypocrisy which is more often
treated by the method of savage caricature. If he is
not as amusing as a Tartuffe or a Pecksniff, he is
marvellously lifelike. Nothing can be finer than the
description of the curious blending of motives and the
ingenious self-deception which enables Bulstrode to
maintain his own self-respect. He is afraid of exposure by the scamp who has known his past history.
" At six o'clock he had already been long dressed, and
had spent some of his wretchedness in prayer, pleading
his motives for averting the worst evil if in anything
he had used falsity and spoken what was not true

before God. For Bulstrode shrank from a direct lie
with an intensity disproportionate to the number of
his direct misdeeds. But many of those misdeeds
were like the subtle muscular movements which are
not taken account of in the consciousness, though they
bring about the end that we fix our mind on and
desire. And it is only what we are naïvely conscious
of that we can vividly imagine to be seen by Omni-
science." The culminating scene in which Bulstrode
comes to the edge of murder, and, though he does not
kill his enemy, refrains from officiously saving life, is
the practical application of the principles; and one is
half inclined to think that there was some excuse for
the proceeding.

It is, I think, to the force and penetration shown in
such passages that *Middlemarch* owes its impressiveness. It shows George Eliot's reflective powers fully
ripened and manifesting singular insight into certain
intricacies of motive and character. There is, indeed,
a correlative loss of the early power of attractiveness.
The remaining pair of lovers, Mary Garth and Fred
Vincy, the shrewd young woman and the feeble young
gentleman whom she governs, do not carry us away;
and Caleb Garth, though he is partly drawn from the
same original as Adam Bede, is unimpeachable, but a
faint duplicate of his predecessor. The moral most
obviously suggested would apparently be that the
desirable thing is to do your work well in the position
to which Providence has assigned you, and not to bother
about "ideals" at all. *Il faut cultiver notre jardin* is
an excellent moral, but it comes more appropriately at
the end of *Candide* than at the end of a story which is
to give us a modern Theresa.

This, I think, explains the rather painful impression which is made by *Middlemarch*. It is prompted by a sympathy for the enthusiast, but turns out to be virtually a satire upon the modern world. The lofty nature is to be exhibited struggling against the circumambient element of crass stupidity and stolid selfishness. But that element comes to represent the dominant and overpowering force. Belief is in so chaotic a state that the idealist is likely to go astray after false lights. Intellectual ambition mistakes pedantry for true learning; religious aspiration tempts acquiescence in cant and superstition; the desire to carry your creed into practice makes compromise necessary, and compromise passes imperceptibly into surrender. One is tempted to ask whether this does not exaggerate one aspect of the human tragicomedy. The unity, to return to our " parable," is to be the light carried by the observer in search of an idealist. In *Middlemarch* the light shows the aspirations of the serious actors, and measures their excellence by their capacity for such a motive. The test so suggested seems to give a rather one-sided view of the world. The perfect novelist, if such a being existed, looking upon human nature from a thoroughly impartial and scientific point of view, would agree that such aspirations are rare and obviously impossible for the great mass of mankind. People, indisputably, are " mostly fools," and care very little for theories of life and conduct. But, therefore, it is idle to quarrel with the inevitable or to be disappointed at its results; and, moreover, it is easy to attach too much importance to this particular impulse. The world, somehow or other, worries along by means of very commonplace affections and very limited outlooks. George Eliot, no doubt, fully recognises that fact, but she seems to be dispirited by the contemplation. The result, however, is that she seems to be a little out of touch with the actual world, and to speak from a position of philosophical detachment which somehow exhibits her characters in a rather distorting light. For that reason *Middlemarch* seems to fall short of the great masterpieces which imply a closer contact with the world of realities and less preoccupation with certain speculative doctrines. Yet it is clearly a work of extraordinary power, full of subtle and accurate observation; and gives, if a melancholy, yet an undeniably truthful portraiture of the impression made by the society of the time upon one of the keenest observers, though upon an observer looking at the world from a certain distance, and rather too much impressed by the importance of philosophers and theorists.

CHAPTER XIII

DANIEL DERONDA

GEORGE ELIOT was to write one more novel, and one which was intended to give most clearly her message to mankind. In June 1874 she is "brewing her future big book." In February 1876 the first part was published; it came out in the same form as *Middlemarch*, in eight monthly parts, and had from the first a larger sale than its predecessor. Here again we have the doctrine of ideals, and expounded with even more emphasis. The story is really two stories put side by side and intersecting at intervals. Each gives a life embodying a principle, and each illustrates its opposite by the contrast. Gwendolen Harleth, a young lady with aspirations in a latent state, is misled into a worldly marriage, and though ultimately saved, is saved "as by fire." Daniel Deronda is throughout true to his higher nature, and is, in George Eliot's works, what Sir Charles Grandison is in Richardson's — the type of human perfection. The story of Gwendolen's marriage shows undiminished power. Here and there, perhaps, we have a little too much psychological analysis; but, after all, the reader who objects to psychology can avoid it by skipping a paragraph or two. It is another version of the old tragic motive: the paralysing influence of unmitigated

and concentrated selfishness, already illustrated by
Tito and Rosamond. Grandcourt, to whom Gwendolen sacrifices herself, is compared to a crab or a
boa-constrictor slowly pinching its victim to death :
to appeal to him for mercy would be as idle as to
appeal to "a dangerous serpent ornamentally coiled
on her arm." He is a Tito in a further stage of
development — with all better feelings atrophied, and
enabled, by his fortune, to gratify his spite without
exerting himself in intrigues. Like Tito, he suggests,
to me at least, rather the cruel woman than the male
autocrat. Some critic remarked, to George Eliot's annoyance, that the scenes between him and his parasite
Lush showed the "imperious feminine, not the masculine character." She comforted herself by the
statement that Bernal Osborne — a thorough man of
the world — had commended these scenes as specially
lifelike. I can, indeed, accept both views, for the
distinction is rather too delicate for definite application. One feels, I think, that Grandcourt was
drawn by a woman; but a sort of voluptuous enjoyment of malignant tyranny is unfortunately not confined to either sex. Anyhow, Gwendolen's ordeal is
pathetic, and she excites more sympathy than any of
George Eliot's victims. Perhaps she excites a little
too much. At least, when she comes very near homi-
cide (like Caterina in the Clerical Scenes and Bulstrode
in *Middlemarch*), and withholds her hand from her
drowning husband, one is strongly tempted to give
the verdict, "Served him right." She, however, feels
some remorse ; and Daniel Deronda, who becomes her
confessor, is much too admirable a being to give any
sanction to this immoral source of consolation. She is

so charming in her way that we feel more interest in
the criminal than in the confessor. " I have no sympathy," she says on one occasion, " with women who
are always doing right."   Perhaps that is the reason
why we cannot quite bow the knee before Daniel
Deronda.

That young gentleman is a model from the first.
He has a " seraphic face."   There is " hardly a delicacy
of feeling " of which he is not capable — even when he
is at Eton.   He is so ethereal a being that we are a
little shocked when he is mentioned in connection with
entrées.   One can't fancy an angel at a London dinner
table.   That is, indeed, the impression which he makes
upon his friend.   A family is created expressly to pay
homage to him.   They are supposed to have a sense of
humour to make their worship more impressive ; but
they certainly keep it in the background when speaking of him.   People, says one of the young ladies,
must be content to take our brothers for husbands,
because they can't get Deronda.   " No woman ought
to want to marry him," replies her sister . . . " fancy
finding out that he had a tailor's bill and used boot-
hooks, like our brother."   Angels don't employ tailors.
They compare him to his face to Buddha, who gave
himself to a famishing tigress to save her and her cubs
from starvation.   To Gwendolen this peerless person
naturally becomes an " outer conscience " ; and when he
exhorts her to use her past sorrow as a preparation for
life, instead of letting it spoil her life, the words are
to her " like the touch of a miraculous hand."   She
begins " a new existence," but it seems " inseparable
from Deronda," and she longs that his presence may
be permanent.   Happily she does not dare to love him,

and hopes only to be bound to him by a "spiritual tie." That is just as well, because by a fortunate accident he has picked a perfect young Jewess out of the Thames, into which she had thrown herself, like Mary Wollstonecraft. Moreover, by another providential accident — Providence interferes rather to excess — he has walked into the city and stumbled upon a virtuous Jewish pawnbroker; and at the pawnbroker's has met the Jewess's long-lost brother Mordecai, who turns out to be as perfect as Deronda himself.

It must be admitted that the Jewish circle into which Deronda is admitted does not strike one as drawn from the life. That is only natural, as Mordecai is the incarnated pursuit of an ideal. Mordecai is devoted to the restoration of the Jewish nationality — a scheme which to the vulgar mind seems only one degree less chimerical than Zarca's plan for a gypsy nationality in Africa. It gives a chance to Deronda, however. For a perfect young man in a time of "social questions," he has hitherto been rather oddly at a loss for an end to which he can devote his powers. This is explained by a lengthy dissertation on his character. He is too good. "His plenteous flexible sympathy had ended by falling into one current with that reflective analysis which tends to neutralise sympathy." He is not vicious, but he "takes even vices mildly"; he is "fervidly democratic" from sympathy with the people, and yet "intensely conservative" from imagination and affection. He likes to be on the losing side in order to have the pleasure of martyrdom; but he is afraid that too much martyrdom will make him bitter. The solution comes by the discovery, strangely delayed by a combination of circumstances,

that he was a genuine Jew by birth. Now he can
accept Mordecai for his prophet and take "heredity"
for his guide. "You," he says to that inspired person,
"have given shape to what, I believe, was an inherited
yearning — the effect of brooding passionate thoughts
in many ancestors — thoughts that seem to have been
intensely present with my grandfather." He has
always longed for an "ideal task" — some "captain-
ship, which should come to him as a duty and not
be striven for as a personal prize." The "idea that
I am possessed with," as he afterward explains, is
"that of restoring a political existence to my people,
making them a nation again, giving them a national
centre such as the English, though they too are
scattered over the face of the globe." It seems from
her volume of essays (*Theophrastus Such*) that George
Eliot considered this to be a reasonable investment
of human energy. As we cannot all discover that
we belong to the chosen people, and some of us might,
even then, doubt the wisdom of the enterprise, one feels
that Deronda's mode of solving his problem is not
generally applicable. George Eliot's sympathy for the
Jews, her aversion to Anti-Semitism, was thoroughly
generous, and naturally welcomed by its objects.
But taken as the motive of a hero it strikes one as
showing a defective sense of humour. "One may
understand jokes without liking them," says the
musician Klesmer; and adds, "I am very sensible
to wit and humour." There can be no doubt that
George Eliot was very sensible to those qualities, and
yet she refuses to perceive that Daniel Deronda is an
amiable monomaniac and occasionally a very prosy
moralist.

I must repeat that George Eliot was intensely feminine, though more philosophical than most women.
She shows it to the best purpose in the subtlety and
the charm of her portraits of women, unrivalled in some
ways by any writer of either sex; and shows it also,
as I think, in a true perception of the more feminine
aspects of her male characters. Still, she sometimes
illustrates the weakness of the feminine view. Daniel
Deronda is not merely a feminine but, one is inclined
to say, a schoolgirl's hero. He is so sensitive and
scrupulously delicate that he will not soil his hands by
joining in the rough play of ordinary political and
social reformers. He will not compromise, and yet he
shares the dislike of his creator for fanatics and the
devotees of "fads." The monomaniac type is certainly
disagreeable, though it may be useful. Deronda con-
trives to avoid its more offensive peculiarities, but at
the price of devoting himself to an unreal and dreamy
object. Probably, one fancies, he became disgusted in
later life by finding that, after Mordecai's death, the
people with whom he had to work had not the charm
of that half-inspired visionary. He is, in any case, an
idealist, who can only be provided with a task by a
kind of providential interposition. The discovery that
one can be carrying out one's grandfather's ideas is
not generally a very powerful source of inspiration.
"Heredity" represents an important factor in life, but
can hardly be made into a religion. So far, therefore,
as Deronda is an æsthetic embodiment of an ethical
revelation — a judicious hint to a young man in search
of an ideal — he represents an untenable theory. From
the point of view of the simple novel reader he fails from
unreality. George Eliot, in later years, came to know

several representatives in the younger generation of the class to which Deronda belonged. She speaks, for example, with great warmth of Henry Sidgwick. His friends, she remarks, by their own account, always "expected him to act according to a higher standard" than they would attribute to any one else or adopt for themselves. She sent Deronda to Cambridge soon after she had written this, and took great care to give an accurate account of the incidents of Cambridge life. I have always fancied — though without any evidence — that some touches in Deronda were drawn from one of her friends, Edmund Gurney, a man of remarkable charm of character, and as good-looking as Deronda. In the Cambridge atmosphere of Deronda's days there was, I think, a certain element of rough common sense which might have knocked some of her hero's nonsense out of him. But, in any case, one is sensible that George Eliot, if she is thinking of real life at all, has come to see through a romantic haze which deprives the portrait of reality. The imaginative sense is declining, and the characters are becoming emblems or symbols of principle, and composed of more moonshine than solid flesh and blood. The Gwendolen story taken by itself is a masterly piece of social satire; but in spite of the approval of learned Jews, it is impossible to feel any enthusiastic regard for Deronda in his surroundings.

CHAPTER XIV

CONCLUSION

THE Leweses had been in the habit of recruiting their health in various country places in the neighbourhood of London, as well as in occasional trips to the Continent. In 1876 they bought a house at Witley, near Godalming, in the charming Surrey country which looks up to Hindhead and Blackdown. They were neighbours of Tennyson, who saw them occasionally both there and in town. An anecdote of a quarrel between them is refuted by Tennyson's son. What really happened was that, as she was leaving his house, Tennyson pressed her hand " kindly and sweetly," and said, " I wish you well with your molecules ! " She replied as gently, " I get on very well with my molecules." Tennyson held that the flight of Hetty in *Adam Bede* and Thackeray's account of Colonel Newcome's decline were " the two most pathetic things in modern fiction." He greatly admired her insight into character, " but did not think her so true to nature as Shakespeare and Miss Austen." I will not argue upon such dicta, though they are interesting in regard to both persons. George Eliot was more or less acquainted with other eminent writers of her time. The Leweses stayed with Mark Pattison at Oxford, and afterwards with

Jowett, who sent them the proof-sheets of his *Plato*.
Dickens was friendly till his death, and she speaks
with affection of Anthony Trollope, "one of the
heartiest, most genuine, and moral men we know."
Their life, however, continued to be secluded, and
they thought of retiring altogether to Witley. Lewes
was now working at his last book, the *Problems of
Life and Mind*, but his health was beginning to break.
He was taken ill at the "Priory" towards the end
of 1878, and died on 28th November.

George Eliot was prostrated by the blow. The
first employment to which she could devote herself
was the arrangement of Lewes's unfinished work.
She resolved to found a "George Henry Lewes
studentship," which should enable some young man
to carry on physiological research. Henry Sidgwick,
Sir Michael Foster, and others gave her advice, and
in the course of the year the plan was settled and a
student elected. Gradually she revived. Her friend,
Madame Bodichon, describes her in June 1879 as
"wretchedly thin" and looking "in her long loose
black dress like the black shadow of herself." Still,
she said that "she had so much to do that she must
keep well"; the world was *so* "intensely interesting."
She had at this time published the last of her books,
which had already been read and approved by Lewes.
The Impressions of Theophrastus Such is a curious performance which certainly seems to suggest that her
intellect — though not weakened — had somehow got
into the least appropriate application of its energies.
A short essay should above all things be bright and
clear, and if it touches grave thoughts, touch them with
a light hand. Nobody can call *Theophrastus Such* light

o

in its touch. The mannerism which showed itself
occasionally in her first works, the ironical application
of scientific analogies to trifling matters, sometimes hits
the mark, but was always apt to become ponderous,
if not pedantic. *Theophrastus Such* seems to be entirely
composed of such matter, questionable, perhaps, at the
best, and making the unpleasant impression of all
laborious attempts at witticism. She had, for example,
been disgusted, as every real lover of good literature
must be disgusted, at flippant and irreverent bur-
lesques. She protests against a practice which she
calls " debasing the moral currency." " And yet, it
seems, parents will put into the hands of their children
ridiculous parodies (perhaps with more ridiculous
' illustrations ') of the poems which stirred their own
tenderness and filial duty, and cause them to make
their first acquaintance with great men, great works,
or solemn crises, through the medium of some miscellaneous burlesque which, with its idiotic puns and
farcical attitudes, will remain among their primary
associations and reduce them throughout their time
of studious preparation for life to the moral imbecility
of an inward giggle at what might have stimulated
the high emulation which fed the fountains of com-
passion, trust, and constancy." That may be very
true, but surely it would be possible to put it a
little more pointedly. George Eliot in writing these
essays seems first to have got into the too didactic vein
to which she was always prone, and then to have put
her observations into the most tortuous and cumbrous
shape by way of giving them an air of solemnity.
What, one asks, had become of Mrs. Poyser ? The
book, however, succeeded well enough to satisfy her ;

but I can hardly believe that anybody can now read it except from a sense of duty.

The remainder of George Eliot's life may be told in a few words. In 1867 Lewes had been introduced by Mr. Herbert Spencer to Mrs. Cross, a lady then living at Weybridge with a daughter, Miss Elizabeth D. Cross, who had just published a volume of poems. Miss Cross was invited by Lewes to see George Eliot, and a friendship sprang up between the families. In 1869 the Leweses paid a visit to the Crosses at Weybridge, and the friendship became intimacy. The death of Lewes's son, Thornton, and of a married daughter of Mrs. Cross within the next two months, strengthened the bond by mutual sympathy. Mr. John Walter Cross, son of Mrs. Cross, then a banker at New York, was staying at Weybridge during George Eliot's visit, and soon afterwards settled in England in his mother's house. He became very intimate with the Leweses, and frequently visited them at Witley. After Lewes's death he was an able and sympathetic adviser. His mother had died a week after Lewes, and he was anxious to find relief and occupation in some new pursuit. He began to read Dante, and George Eliot proposed to help him in his studies. From that time they saw each other constantly; and as George Eliot's spirit recovered from the shock, she began again to find pleasure in music and in visiting the National Gallery. The support of Mr. Cross's companionship relieved her sense of desolation, and in April 1880 they decided upon marriage. The marriage took place on 6th May, and the only possible comment is her own statement to Mme. Bodichon. "Mr. Cross's family," she says, "welcome me with the utmost ten-

derness. All this is wonderful blessing falling to me
beyond my share after I had thought that life was
ended, and that, so to speak, my coffin was ready for
me in the next room. Deep down below there is a
river of sadness, but this must always be with those
who have lived long — and I am able to enjoy my
newly reopened life. I shall be a better, more loving
creature than I could have been in solitude. To be
constantly, lovingly grateful for the gift of a perfect
love is the best illumination of one's mind to all the
possible good there may be in store for man on this
troublous little planet."

The Crosses made a tour after their marriage, staying some time at Venice, and returning to Witley by
the end of July. Her health seemed at first to have
greatly improved, and she was able to take walks and
to see sights during the journey. After returning to
England, she had a serious attack in September, followed by a partial recovery. On 4th December the
Crosses moved into a new house which they had taken
at 4 Cheyne Walk, Chelsea. A fortnight later a slight
chill brought on a fresh attack. Her previous illness
had weakened her power of rallying, and she died on
22nd December 1880.

George Eliot's main personal characteristics should
be sufficiently indicated by what I have already said.
A few remarks, however, may help to complete the
picture. Among her active employments she found
time to lead the life of an industrious student. Though
frequently interrupted by ill-health, she was capable
of sustained and severe attention to difficult subjects.
The list of her accomplishments acquired at different
periods is a long one. She had a thorough knowledge

of French, German, Italian, and Spanish, and could talk in each language correctly, though "with difficulty." She could read the classical languages with pleasure; and kept up her familiarity with the great masterpieces of all periods by frequent re-reading. She was fond of reading aloud, especially Milton and the Bible; and a fine voice, perfectly under command, gave peculiar power to her rendering of solemn and majestic passages. Hebrew was a favourite study; and though she read little of the lighter literature of the day, she had a very retentive memory of the novels — George Sand's, for example — which she had read in her youth. She read a good many historical works, and, as we have seen, could get up minute antiquarian details with unflagging industry. Besides her main studies, she had dipped into scientific writings, had at one time taken to geometry, and thought that she had some aptitude for mathematics. Her interest in the philosophical speculations of the time we have sufficiently indicated. Her powers of assimilating knowledge were, in fact, extraordinary, and it may safely be said that no novelist of mark ever possessed a wider intellectual culture. With all her knowledge, she attended to the ordinary feminine duties. She was proud of her good housekeeping, and her early training and love of order had given her a thorough knowledge of how such matters should be done. She sympathised, of course, with projects for reforming female education, and was one of the first subscribers to Girton College. She had, however, a characteristic misgiving lest a university system might weaken the bonds of family life. The feminine qualities are as characteristic of the student as of the writer. She read reverently, with a desire to appreciate and admire. The critical, or rather scoffing attitude of mind, was intensely antipathetic to her. She seems to have loved especially the gentler and more serious observers of life, such as Goldsmith and Cowper and Miss Austen, and venerated such great men as Dante and Milton (" her demi-god," as she calls him), whose austerity breathes a lofty moral sentiment. She rarely expresses her antipathies; but one instance is characteristic. Of Byron she speaks with disgust, as the " most vulgar-minded genius that ever produced a great effect in literature." The author of *Don Juan* could not well be congenial to the creator of Fedalma. Women, it is said, are wanting in humour; and perhaps for the obvious reason that the humorist is apt to find that the easiest roads of making a point lie through profanity or indecency. George Eliot's sense of humour was undeniably keen, but she will not give play to it when it takes the offensive. That need not be regretted. It is a less satisfactory result when her desire to sympathise with all high impulses leads her in her later stories to shut her eyes to the comic side, which forces itself upon the less restrained humorists, and to present us with model characters verging too decidedly upon priggishness. A touch of pedagogic severity saddens her view of the frivolous world. Her profound conviction of the mischief done by stupidity, of the clogging and degrading effect of the general atmosphere of commonplace upon aspiring souls, diminishes her appreciation of fools, and *Theophrastus Such* suggests even a tinge of sourness. George Eliot, we are told, took little interest in contemporary politics. During the war of 1870 she reminds a friend of the

famous anecdote of Goethe's indifference to the Revolution of 1830 as compared with the controversies of
Cuvier and Saint-Hilaire. She says that it is impossible
to "doff aside" the French and German war after that
fashion. In general, however, she seems to have
accepted Goethe's attitude, and to have been more
interested in the advances of scientific thought than
in the reforming energies of Gladstone's first government. She thought that political matters in England
were managed by "amateurs," that their quarrels
involved a growing quantity of personal abuse and im-
putation of unworthy motive. That is a natural impression of the philosophical looker-on; and I need not ask
whether active politicians are justified in meeting it
with simple contempt. Her sympathy with the positivists predisposed her, moreover, to think more of
the slow operation of changed ideals than of particular
political changes. Her interest in positivism was
always strong. She was on terms of intimate friendship with Dr. Congreve, Mr. Frederic Harrison, and
Professor Beesly, and subscribed to the funds of the
central body. She did not, indeed, accept positivist
doctrines unreservedly, and had by her side a keen
critic in George Lewes, who had followed Comte's
early teaching, but repudiated the theories of social
reconstruction propounded in the later *Politique Posi-
tive*. Both, it appears, regarded it as "a Utopia, pre-
senting hypotheses rather than doctrines," and she
could sympathise with Comte as "an individual"
trying "to anticipate the work of future generations."
The special point of sympathy was, of course, the
aspect with which the Comtists regarded the old
creeds as stages in the continuous evolution of

humanity. In that respect, too, George Eliot was eminently feminine. She had the strong religious instinct common to so many noble women in whose sympathy masculine reformers have found comfort amidst the harsh controversies and struggles of active work. The history of her books is on one side a history of the consequent development of her mind. Her intellectual expansion led her to accept the teaching of the men who represented for her the most advanced thought of the time. But the aggressiveness which it generated for a time was a transitory frame of mind. The first series of novels represents the fond dwelling upon all the loftier impulses which had uttered themselves in stammering and imperfect dialects prescribed by dogmas no longer tenable; while the later correspond to a longing to find an utterance reconcilable with full acceptance of scientific truth. Daniel Deronda, one fancies, would have embodied her sentiments more completely if, instead of devoting himself to the Jews, he had become a leading prophet in the church of humanity. That, no doubt, would have brought him into too close a contact with notorious facts.

I have said that George Eliot's peculiar place among the novelists of the time was in some sense determined by the philosophical tendencies which were shared by none of her contemporaries. I do not mean to imply that it was her proper function to propagate any philosophical doctrine, and have tried to point out the defects due to her inclinations in that direction. Novels should, I take it, be transfigured experience; they should be based upon the direct observation and the genuine emotions which it has inspired: when they are deliberately intended to be a symbolism of any general formula, they become unreal as representative of fact, and unsatisfactory as philosophical exposition. George Eliot's early success and the faults of her later work illustrate, I have said, the right and wrong methods. But, in conclusion, I may try to indicate what seems to me to be the quality which, in spite of inevitable shortcomings in undertaking the impossible, gives the permanent interest of her works. That, I think, appears most simply by regarding them as implicit autobiography. George Eliot gives a direct picture of the England of her early days, and, less directly, a picture of its later developments. Her picture of the old country life owes its charm to the personal memories, and may possibly have a little personal colouring. If a novelist could be thoroughly "realistic," and give the truth, the whole truth, and nothing but the truth, there would no doubt be a good deal to add to the descriptions of the life at Shepperton and Dorlcote Mill. But then, I do not believe that any human intellect can give the whole truth about anything. What can be given truly is the impression made upon the mind of the observer; and when the observer has a mind of such reflective power, so much insight, and such tenderness and sensibility as George Eliot's, its impressions will correspond to realities, and reveal most interesting though not all-comprehensive truths. The combination of an exquisitely sympathetic and loving nature with a large and tolerant intellect is manifest throughout. George Eliot could see the absurdities, and even the brutalities, of her neighbours plainly, but understood them well enough to make them intelligible, not mere absurdities to be caricatured;

she saw the charming aspects of the old order with
equal clearness, but has no illusions which would
convert the country into a pretty Arcadia; and
her sympathy with sorrow and unsatisfied longings
is too deep and reflective to allow her to stray into
mere sentimentalism. Her pathos is powerful because
it is always under command. The more superficial
writer treats an era of misery as implying a grievance
which can be summarily removed, or finds in it an
opportunity of exhibiting his own sensibility. Her
feeling is too deep and her perception of the complexity of its causes too thorough to admit of such
treatment. We see the tender woman who has gone
through much experience, always devotedly attached
by the strongest ties of affection ; but always reflecting,
shrinking from excesses of passion or of scoffing, and
trying to see men and life as parts of a wider order.

The same personal element appears in her later
work in spite of the defects which I take to be undeniable. George Eliot, as we have seen, looked on
the world with a certain aloofness. She read little of
the ephemeral literature of the day, and apparently
thought very ill of what she did read. She looked at
the political warfare from a distance, and did not go
into the society deeply interested in such matters. The
" Priory " was frequented by a circle whose talk was of
philosophy and scientific discoveries, and which was
more interested in theories than in the gossip of the
day. She had not therefore the experience which could
enable her to describe contemporary life, with its
social and political ambitions and the rough struggle
for existence in which practical lawyers and men of
business are mainly occupied. She thinks of the

world chiefly as the surrounding element of sordid aims into which her idealists are to go forth with such hope as may be of leavening the mass. She could not, therefore, draw lifelike portraits of such characters as were the staple of the ordinary novelist. The questions, however, in which she was profoundly interested were undeniably of the highest importance. The period of her writings was one in which, as we can now see more clearly than at the time, very significant changes were taking place in English thought and life. Controversies on " evolutionism" and socialism and democracy were showing the set of the current. George Eliot's heroes and heroines are all more or less troubled by the results, whether they live ostensibly in England or in distant countries and centuries. I need say nothing more of her special view of the questions at issue. But incidentally, as one may say, she came, in treating of her favourite theme — the idealist in search of a vocation — to exhibit her own characteristics. The long gallery of heroines, from Milly Barton to Gwendolen Harleth, have various tasks set to them, in which we may be more or less interested. But the women themselves, whatever their outward circumstances, have an interest unsurpassed by any other writer. They have, of course, a certain family likeness; and if Maggie is most like her creator, the others show an affinity to some of her characteristics. George Eliot is reported to have said that the character which she found most difficult to support was that of Rosamond Vincy, the young woman who paralyses Lydgate. One can understand the statement, for it is Rosamond's function to do exactly what is most antipathetic to her biographer.

She is the embodied contradictory of her creator's morality. Yet she, too, is a vigorous portrait, and the whole series may be given triumphantly as a proof of what is called "knowledge of the human heart." I dislike the phrase, because it seems to imply that an abstract science with that subject-matter is in existence — which I should certainly deny. But if it only means that George Eliot could — without any formula — sympathise with a singularly wide range of motive and feeling, and especially with noble and tender natures, and represent the concrete embodiment with extraordinary power, then I can fully subscribe to the opinion. I think, as I have said, that one is always conscious that her women are drawn from the inside, and that her most successful men are substantially women in disguise. But the two sexes have a good deal in common; and in the setting forth some of the moral and intellectual processes which we can all understand, George Eliot shows unsurpassable skill. Here and there, no doubt, there is too much explicit "psychological analysis," and a rather ponderous enumeration of obvious aphorisms in the pomp of scientific analogy. But she is singularly powerful in describing the conflicts of emotions; the ingenious modes of self-deception in which most of us acquire considerable skill; the uncomfortable results of keeping a conscience till we have learnt to come to an understanding with it; the grotesque mixture of motives which results when we have reached a *modus vivendi;* the downright hypocrisy of the lower nature, or the comparatively pardonable and even commendable state of mind of the person who has a thoroughly consistent code of action, though he unconsciously interprets its

laws in a non-natural sense to suit his convenience.
George Eliot's power of watching and describing the
various manœuvres by which people keep their self-
respect and satisfy their feelings shows her logical
subtlety, which appears again in her quaint description
of the odd processes which take the place of reasoning
in the uneducated intelligence.

George Eliot believed that a work of art not only
may, but must, exercise also an ethical influence. I
will not inquire how much influence is actually
exerted by novels upon the morality of their readers ;
but so far as any influence is exerted, it is due, I think,
in the last resort to the personality of the novelist.
That is to say, that from reading George Eliot's novels
we are influenced in the same way as by an intimacy
with George Eliot herself. Undoubtedly, in effect,
that might vary indefinitely according to the prejudices and character of the other party. But, in any
case, we feel that the writer with whom we have been
in contact possessed a singularly wide and reflective
intellect, a union of keen sensibility with a thoroughly
tolerant spirit, a desire to appreciate all the good
hidden under the commonplace and narrow, a lively
sympathy with all the nobler aspirations, a vivid
insight into the perplexities and delusions which beset
even the strongest minds, brilliant powers of wit, at
once playful and pungent, and, if we must add, a rather
melancholy view of life in general, a melancholy
which is not nursed for purposes of display, but forced
upon a fine understanding by the view of a state of
things which, we must admit, does not altogether lend
itself to a cheerful optimism. I have endeavoured to
point out what limitations must be adopted by an

honest critic.   George Eliot's works, as I have read,
have not, at the present day, quite so high a position
as was assigned to them by contemporary enthusiasm.
That is a common phenomenon enough ; and, in her
case, I take it to be due chiefly to the partial mis-
direction of her powers in the later period.   But when I
compare her work with that of other novelists, I cannot
doubt that she had powers of mind and a richness of
emotional nature rarely equalled, or that her writings —
whatever their shortcomings — will have a corresponding value in the estimation of thoughtful readers.